The Inward Ear

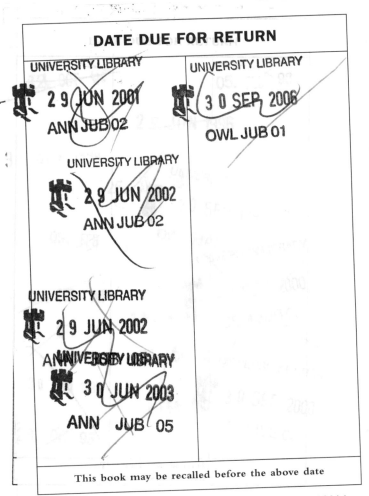

CAMBRIDGE HANDBOOKS FOR LANGUAGE TEACHERS
General Editor: Michael Swan

This is a series of practical guides for teachers of English and other languages. Illustrative examples are usually drawn from the field of English as a foreign or second language, but the ideas and techniques described can equally well be used in the teaching of any language.

In this series:

Drama Techniques in Language Learning – A resource book of communication activities for language teachers
by Alan Maley and Alan Duff

Games for Language Learning
by Andrew Wright, David Betteridge and Michael Buckby

Discussions that Work – Task-centred fluency practice *by Penny Ur*

Once Upon a Time – Using stories in the language classroom
by John Morgan and Mario Rinvolucri

Teaching Listening Comprehension *by Penny Ur*

Keep Talking – Communicative fluency activities for language teaching
by Friederike Klippel

Working with Words – A guide to teaching and learning vocabulary
by Ruth Gairns and Stuart Redman

Learner English – A teacher's guide to interference and other problems
edited by Michael Swan and Bernard Smith

Testing Spoken Language – A handbook of oral testing techniques
by Nic Underhill

Literature in the Language Classroom – A resource book of ideas and activities *by Joanne Collie and Stephen Slater*

Dictation – New methods, new possibilities
by Paul Davis and Mario Rinvolucri

Grammar Practice Activities – A practical guide for teachers *by Penny Ur*

Testing for Language Teachers *by Arthur Hughes*

The Inward Ear – Poetry in the language classroom
by Alan Maley and Alan Duff

Pictures for Language Learning *by Andrew Wright*

The Inward Ear

Poetry in
the language classroom

Alan Maley
and Alan Duff

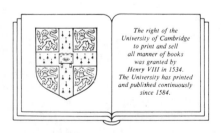

The right of the
University of Cambridge
to print and sell
all manner of books
was granted by
Henry VIII in 1534.
The University has printed
and published continuously
since 1584.

Cambridge University Press
Cambridge
New York   Port Chester
Melbourne   Sydney

348998

Published by the Press Syndicate of the University of Cambridge
The Pitt Building, Trumpington Street, Cambridge CB2 1RP
40 West 20th Street, New York, NY 10011, USA
10 Stamford Road, Oakleigh, Melbourne 3166, Australia

© Cambridge University Press 1989

First published 1989
Reprinted 1990

Printed in Great Britain by Bell & Bain Ltd, Glasgow

Library of Congress cataloguing in publication data

Maley, Alan, 1937–
The inward ear: poetry in the language classroom/Alan Maley and Alan Duff.
       p.   cm. – (Cambridge handbooks for language teachers)
Bibliography: p.
Includes index.
ISBN 0-521-32048-8. – ISBN 0-521-31240-X (pbk.)
1. Language and languages – Study and teaching. 2. Poetry – Study
and teaching.   I. Duff, Alan, 1942–   . II. Title.   III. Series.
P53.M26 1989
808.1–dc20   89-9922 CIP

British Library cataloguing in publication data

Maley, Alan
The inward ear: poetry in the language classroom.
(Cambridge handbooks for language teachers)
1. Educational institutions. Curriculum subjects:
English language. Teaching
I. Title II. Duff, Alan
420'.7

ISBN 0 521 32048 8 hard covers
ISBN 0 521 31240 X paperback

WD

Contents

For Viva

Thanks

We would like to thank all those students, teachers and friends who have contributed to the making of this book. In particular we are grateful to Michael Swan for his invaluable help, encouragement and inspiration.

About the book – notes to the user

These notes are designed to meet some of the questions which may arise when working with poetry, and to offer some practical suggestions for using the book.

More detailed *comments* and specific instructions for *what to do* in each activity are given in the main body of the book. Here we are concerned with the general approach.

At the end of the book, a brief outline is given of how activities might be combined to make up 'an hour's work'.

Who is it for?

The Inward Ear is a handbook for teachers of English as a foreign language. It is based on the use of poetry in language learning, and provides a wide range of activities suitable for students of both *language* and *literature*. It may be used as supplementary course material or as the basis for intensive language practice, e.g. on teacher training courses.

All students from secondary school level upwards will be able to work with the activities described in *The Inward Ear*. It should be stressed that neither students nor teachers require any formal background in literature.

Level

The material in this book has not been graded according to language level – but it has been carefully selected. The poems chosen as examples are ones which we felt a foreign learner of English could understand, and appreciate, *without undue difficulty*.

The poems, however, have not been matched against any lexical or structural lists. Students will undoubtedly come across unknown words – such as, *clematis*, *martyrdom* or *conversation-piece* – but unknown words can be explained, or discovered from the context, or through discussion. A poem is not necessarily too 'advanced' because it contains unknown words.

Poems do not conform to artificially devised language 'levels'. Nor can they be edited to make them conform. The teacher must therefore use his

1

or her own sensibility in deciding which poems in the book are suitable for a particular class. It is important for the teacher to keep clearly in mind the distinction between *techniques* which may be applied to poems at any level, and *texts* which are necessarily at a given level.

As far as the exercises are concerned, the language level will be determined by the students' ability. Matching a picture with a poem, for instance, is an exercise which can be done by students of all levels from pre-intermediate to advanced. How well they do it will depend on how well they can handle the language. But they will all be *able* to do it – in their own way.

In short, what the students are doing here is what they will be doing in life – finding their own level.

How the book is arranged

The arrangement of the material is determined by the nature of the book. *The Inward Ear* is not a book *about* poetry, or about the teaching of poetry. It is, simply, a book in which poetry is used as a resource – like any other material – for *language practice*. In this sense, the poem serves much the same purpose as, say, a scientific text, a newspaper article, a recorded interview, or any of the other varieties of language commonly found in text-books.

The material is divided into eight chapters, each illustrating particular ways in which poetry can be used. For writing, listening, speaking, for dramatisation and adaptation, etc. The individual poems are given as *examples* of what might be used in a particular activity. But, as we said earlier, they are not tied down to that activity. Other poems could be used, and the same poem could be approached using different techniques. The chapters then, should not be seen as watertight compartments. Ideas flow from one to the other.

Each chapter is introduced by a brief outline of the purpose of the activities. The *activities* themselves are presented as follows:

WHAT TO DO Here we describe, step-by-step, how the exercise is performed. The instructions are directed to the teacher. A sample poem or fragment is given as an illustration of the material needed.

COMMENTS These offer the teacher suggestions for:
a) ways of adapting the exercise,
b) approaches to particular aspects of the poem, e.g. lines which may give difficulty,
c) possible combinations with other activities.

The COMMENTS also help to clarify the purpose of the activity as a *language* exercise.

It is important to remember that the structure of the book is *flexible*.

2

Teachers should feel free to switch from one chapter to another and to combine activities from different parts of the book.

About the activities

We said earlier that one of the aims of the book was to give practice in the *use* of language. This means practice in all four skills. Many of the activities involve a *combination* of skills. For instance, in Tangles (2.12) or Word webs (6.1), the student will be involved in listening or reading, writing, and speaking (discussing).

The aim of the activities is of course to move beyond the mere exercise of skills. As they become involved in genuine interaction focused on meaning, so the students forget, temporarily at least, about language.

It can be fairly said, then, that in using poetry the students are using all their resources.

Working in pairs and groups

Most of the work is done in pairs or in small groups. One of the reasons for this is that the ideas seem to flow best when they are exchanged. Working alone, the student has no outlet for his or her thoughts, as part of a large group, no opportunity to express them. In small groups, it is possible to talk, and to listen. In the activities, students are often asked to change groups and exchange ideas. This helps to keep ideas on the move and prevent the group from 'getting stuck'.

Although we have not said much about *individual* work, this is not to be discounted. Many of the activities can be developed as written exercises, with students working on their own after classes.

Writing

Teachers may be surprised at the importance given to writing in this book. 'Surely students do not need to know how to *write* poetry in English?!' No, they don't. But it is not the primary purpose of the exercises to teach them how to write poetry. The writing is, in fact, an anchor for the discussion. A means of holding down thoughts which are, in fact, expressed *in prose*. A good example is 'The thinginess of things' (6.8), in which the students write down true statements about whatever 'thing' they have chosen, e.g. *mirror*:

> A mirror is made of glass.
> You cannot see through a mirror.
> A mirror only looks one way.

When they come to make their poem, they are actually re-shaping, condensing, their own prose. And also, reformulating their ideas. This is something every language learner needs to be able to do. Writing, as we understand it here, is not writing Poetry (with a capital *P*), but writing down thoughts in the form of a poem. Just as students are asked to write their thoughts in the form of a summary, an essay, or a letter.

And, finally, writing is not seen here as an isolated skill – it is linked to all the others.

Timing

The activities vary greatly in length. Some take as little as a minute, others may last half an hour. Wherever possible, we have given an indication of the average time required. But groups work at different speeds, and their pace is the best indicator.

However, it is not wise to let things simply take their own course. If the students are not given a notional time-limit they will find it difficult to shape their work. They should be told in advance how long they have for a particular exercise. (The teacher may allow some leeway, depending on how the exercise goes, but the instruction should be clear: 'You have seven minutes'. Otherwise, the students will never be ready.)

Most exercises involve several stages: noting ideas, comparing with a partner, expanding and refining, comparing with others, and producing a piece of writing. A typical example of this process is Tangles (2.12), in which the students first devise phrases of their own based on words from the poems, then compare their phrases, and finally come to the poems themselves. If too much time is allowed for the first stage, the final stage will be hurried over and the point of the exercise lost. It is necessary, therefore, to keep the pace fairly brisk in the early stages. You may also need to remind the students that they are not required to produce polished work but to get their ideas down.

The advantage of working in pairs is that those who finish first can compare their ideas, while the others continue working. And so, to some extent, each pair can work at its own speed.

Combining activities

All the activities are complete in themselves, and all can be combined with others. In the COMMENTS, we have indicated some of the most effective combinations. But these are guidelines, not prescriptions. Teachers should not hesitate to adapt the material in their own way.

In An hour's work (see p. 179), we show how different exercises could be combined to make up a whole lesson. However, teachers may often wish to draw on the material to 'fill in a gap' of fifteen to twenty minutes.

Exercises suitable for this purpose can be found in all chapters.

Finally, the question of *themes*. In chapter 2, we have given examples of how two themes – conversation and concentration – could be explored in depth; and in chapters 5 to 8 we have suggested other themes, e.g. loneliness, boredom, happiness etc. In the COMMENTS, we have indicated other themes which might be followed up, for instance: *the senses* – Colours (8.3, 4), Smells (8.5), 'I like that stuff' (5.7), Sounds (1.3), etc.

One of the great values of this material is that it can be approached freshly from different points of view. We hope that teachers will find themes in this book that we have not mentioned.

The poems

Our selection is based mainly on the poetry of this century. This does not mean that poems from the standard anthologies could not also be used. In many of the exercises, e.g. Contrasts (2.14, 15, 16) teachers could make use of poems with which the students are already familiar. Likewise, *prose passages* from text-books could also be used in conjunction with poems, along the lines suggested in, e.g. Interviews (3.7) and Word portraits (3.9).

As a further source of material, teachers might also consider *translations* – or prose versions in English – of poems from the mother tongue.

In the Bibliography, suggestions are given for useful sourcebooks. One of these, Alan Maley and Sandra Moulding's *Poem into Poem* is a students' book which can be used as a companion to *The Inward Ear*.

It is hoped that teachers will look for their own material to use with the activities in this book. In searching for suitable poems it is worth remembering that the material is intended primarily for a *language* class, not for a course in literary appreciation. A poem does not always have to be 'good' (whatever that may mean!) in order to be useful.

Nor does the teacher need to be a poet in order to use poetry.

Introduction

Why use poetry?

'Once upon a time there were three bears: Father Bear, Mother Bear, and Baby Bear . . . ' From our earliest childhood we are exposed to the rhythm and cadence of poetic language. And the primitive power of such language continues to flow as a deep undercurrent through the rest of our lives. Without being aware of it, we respond.

A moment's thought reveals how pervasive this subliminal appeal is in our everyday lives: through political slogans, advertisements/advertising jingles, pop/folk songs, book titles, proverbs and sayings, popular catch phrases, and the like. For instance: *Ban the Bomb*; *Don't be Vague, Ask for Haig*; *This is Your Post Office – Use it or Lose it!*; *We all live in a Yellow Submarine*; *I know where I'm going, I know who's going with me*; *The Jewel in the Crown*; *A Tale of Two Cities*; *a miss is as good as a mile*; *two's company, three's a crowd*.

People seem to be constantly striving for order and pattern. One of the ways they do this is by imposing satisfying patterns on undifferentiated experience.

Yet, for many years now, literature and in particular poetry has not been regarded as 'proper' material for foreign language learning. The whole thrust of the structuralist approach tended to exclude literature except in the form of simplified readers, and the utilitarian bias of the communicative approach deflected attention away from anything which did not seem to have a practical purpose.

Of course, literature continues to be included in some foreign language programmes. But in what form? Unfortunately, all too often it has survived in a traditional mould which is no longer consonant with the rapid changes which have taken place in mainstream Language Teaching. The emphasis remains on the use of texts for commentary and analysis – or merely for illustration. Little attempt is made to help the student to go beyond the mere answering of questions to a discovery of what it is in literature – and specifically in poetry – that lies beyond questions. And it is rare to find poetry integrated into the rest of the student's language learning process. Poetry, if it is included at all, tends to be treated as a slightly anachronistic side-show run by a poor relation.

As a result of all this and, possibly, because of the way in which poetry has been taught in the mother tongue, both teachers and students view poetry with feelings ranging from slight misgiving to downright dislike.

Even when teachers (to their surprise) find that they have used a poem successfully, they are unable to capitalise on this success and take the process a stage further. In short, poetry for them is simply an optional extra rather than an integral part of the language programme.

Whenever the poem is seen in isolation, then, two extreme attitudes emerge: a) The poem is 'a rare flower' – an orchid – to be admired but not touched, or b) The poem is 'a thorn in the flesh', a bothersome text in odd language, involving a ritual of tedious questions which merely slow up the learning.

We would like to suggest that: *Poetry offers a rich resource for input to language learning. As such it is at least as relevant as the more commonly accepted types of input (e.g. contrived dialogues, isolated texts for reading comprehension, simulations, etc.). So, it should be given at least equal weight.*

As will be demonstrated in later sections, the use of a poem as the centrepiece of a unit of material does not preclude the use of other types of language in relation to it. Quite the reverse, in fact. For example, the language used to agree and disagree about 'meaning' in a poem will not be fundamentally different from the language of discussion integral to any interactional activity. The fact that it is a poem rather than a news article that gives rise to the discussion is in this sense relatively unimportant. Many of the activities suggested later are, in fact, only particular forms of problem-solving or information-gap activities.

We believe, too, that if poetry is integrated with other forms of language, and thus demystified through a 'hands-on' approach, students will come to an understanding of what is special about poetry as a mode of language use. And to the further understanding that it is no more 'special' than any other forms of language (e.g. sports reports, advertisements, labels, etc.).

It should be clear by now that we are not advocating a refurbished version of approaches which have traditionally treated the text as a corpse for dissection and post-mortem examination. We would prefer to see it as a living/vital organism which produces lively offspring in the form of other language activities.

>>>→

Poetry's unique advantages

Let us now consider in more detail the advantages which poetry seems to offer.

Universality

Poetry as a form of language use is universal among all human beings. No known language is without it.

On the one hand, the *themes* which poetry deals with are common to all cultures, although the way they are treated naturally differs. *Love, death, nature, children, religious belief, despair* . . . , the list is familiar.

On the other, the *conventions* governing the language of poetry are likewise familiar: *rhythm, rhyme, metre, alliteration, assonance, figurative usage, unusual collocations, elliptic expressions, repetition/refrain* . . . All of these and more are readily recognisable to foreign language learners from their mother-tongue experience.

So, no foreign language learner will be ignorant of what poetry is. What will be unfamiliar is the foreign language code. In other words, though they may not know the language, they will know the conventions. To this extent, poetry is familiar ground.

Non-triviality

Certain kinds of language-teaching materials run the risk of being excessively 'committed', or serious in intent. Others go to the opposite extreme, trivialising the content for the sake of highlighting the language. Students may rapidly lose interest if exposed to a surfeit of rapes, abortions, drugs and bombs, or to the present continuous, the conditional, and direct questions wrapped up in an anodyne content.

It is in the nature of poetry to deal with important experiences (*love, death*, etc.) and to heighten our perception not only of such experiences, but also of the seemingly trivial or unimportant.

> To see a World in a Grain of Sand
> And Heaven in a wild Flower
> Hold Infinity in the Palm of your Hand
> And Eternity in an Hour.
>
> (Blake)

Since poetry deals with important experiences and heightens our awareness of even the apparently trivial, we feel that it provides a content which will appeal to learners because they are able to respond to it in their own way.

Motivation

The fact that the student can make a personal response is in itself a motivating factor. And given that no single interpretation will ever be wholly satisfactory, each individual student can feel that he or she has a valid contribution to make. (Consider, for example, the multiple interpretations of a line such as 'Death, once dead, there's no more dying then' – Shakespeare.)

At first sight poetry in the foreign language may appear impenetrable; however, as we have seen, the student is already familiar from the mother tongue with the conventions of poetry. This makes poetry more readily accessible to him or her. Moreover, the realisation that, though they may be relatively inexpert in the language, they can still appreciate (to a degree) what is thought to be a 'difficult' use of language – and even to write such language – is a far from negligible morale-booster.

Hands on

One of the most important conditions for learning a foreign language (or in developing confidence in one's own language, for that matter) is the opportunity to play with it, to pull it this way and that, to test its elasticity, to test and explore its limits. Poetry is par excellence the medium in which this can be done. (All poets stretch the language in this way: by coining new words, creating new collocations, experimenting with sound, using old words in new ways, and so on.) Learners can not only observe and share the experience of what others have dared to do with the language (e.g. e. e. cummings, *he sang his didn't, he danced his did*), but through interactive writing tasks they can also reach out for the limits of the possible themselves. In one sense, the writing of poetry is an ideal task for language learners because of its tolerance of 'error' (see Widdowson, 1982). This is the sand-pit where guiltless children (and adults too) can try out their constructions.

One further advantage of this 'hands on' approach is that it helps· to remove some of the awe and reverence with which words tend to be surrounded. The student is transformed from a spectator into a participant.

Ambiguity and interaction

Almost without exception, any poem means more than one thing. In many poems there is a core of meaning about which most people would agree (e.g. Keats' *Ode to a Nightingale* is to a nightingale, not to a sparrow!). But a poem may also suggest individual interpretations which are not necessarily shared by all readers. Poems, then, offer both a public and a personal face.

Introduction

Because they are highly suggestive, colourful and associative, poems speak subtly different messages to different people. This is true even of apparently 'simple' material, like nursery-rhymes. The associations called up by a line such as 'The mouse ran up the clock' will be different for different readers, as will the mental image they form.

In teaching, this is an enormous advantage. It means that, within limits, each learner's personal interpretation has validity. It also means that, because each person's perception is different, an almost infinite fund of interactive discussion is possible. The very fact that no two people will have a totally convergent interpretation sets up the tension necessary for a genuine exchange of ideas.

It is, of course, true that discussion can be stimulated in other ways (use of pictures, drama techniques, comprehension texts, etc.). But we feel that, whereas such techniques have already been thoroughly explored, *poetry* – with its peculiar power to stimulate – has been largely neglected.

Reactions and personal relevance

In a recent book (Brown and Yule, 1983), spoken language uses are divided into 'interactional' and 'transactional'. In interactive language use, people are mainly concerned with social lubrication – making speakers feel comfortable with each other. In transactional language, the major concern is with communicating a utilitarian message – giving instructions, offering opinions, making descriptions, etc.

Poetry offers access to a third type of spoken language use which we may call 'reactional'. The main purpose here is neither to make people feel comfortable nor to procure a utilitarian result; rather, to make them react personally to other people's ways of seeing things. All literature does this of course, but poetry has the advantage of doing it very economically.

This development of a personalised reaction to texts – i.e. one which engages not only the intellect but also the feelings – is we feel a very important part of the language learning process.

Memorability

Poems we have read and enjoyed – or rather fragments of them – tend to stick in our minds. This may be because certain phrases are particularly striking or colourful, or because a marked rhyme or an emphatic rhythm has impressed them upon our minds. Very often, they go on repeating themselves in our inward ear and even in our sleep without our consciously trying to recall them. This is no less true of foreign languages than it is of the mother tongue. Such nuggets very often remain in the pool of memory long after communicative competence has drained away.

No-one would wish to claim that these random fragments are of immediate use in other language contexts. Indeed, it would be odd to encounter someone whose speech was punctuated by fragments of poetry. What seems more likely is that they resemble jottings in a mental notebook which occasionally falls open at the right page. In other words, they appear to form a loosely co-ordinated system of unconscious or barely conscious memories which enables the learner to retrieve grammatical and lexical information he or she did not know they had. [To cite just some instances from our own experiences: (subjunctive) *Quand je meurs, je veux qu'on m'enterre . . .* (When I die I want to be buried in . . .) or *Pourtant, il faut il faut que l'on vous dise . . .* (Yet, I'm afraid I have to tell you . . .); (case endings) *Reiten, reiten, reiten, durch den Tag, durch die Nacht . . .* (Riding, riding, riding, through the day, through the night . . .) (Rilke); (conditional) *Had we but world enough and time . . .* (Marvell).]

While we would not wish to lay stress on the conscious memorisation of poetry, it would be a pity not to take advantage of this natural ability to unconsciously absorb language through poetry.

Rhythm

As we have already mentioned, one reason for the relatively easy retention of poetry is its rhythmic appeal. Although it is true that rhythm in poetry does not always follow colloquial speech rhythms, there is very often a clear echo of the everyday spoken language, e.g. *All the world's a stage. And all the men and women merely players . . .* ; *I am sick. I must die. Lord Have Mercy on Us.* And even when common speech rhythms do not seem to be reflected, they still conform to the underlying stress-timed nature of English: a kind of underlying heart-beat. For instance, Hopkins' lines: *O the mind, the mind has mountains.*

According to Brown (1977), rhythm 'is not something extra . . . it is the guide to the structure of information in the spoken message'. In view of this fact, the valuable – perhaps unique – resource which poetry offers should surely be put to use.

Stress and rhythm are often taught through the imitation of model sentences. Our experience, however, inclines us to believe that students are more likely to retain stress and rhythm through exposure to poetry. Even though poetry may not focus expressly on rhythm, it can help develop a sensitivity towards it.

Performance

There are very few occasions when the written word can be spoken naturally, especially in choral form. Poetry, however, offers a ready-made opportunity for such participation. Unlike other forms of choral repetition which are all too often lack-lustre and contrived, poetry can be read aloud by groups without it seeming to be unnatural. And the fact that

11

group performance masks individual imperfections adds to self-confidence.

We have also noticed that not only groups, but individuals too, can be relatively uninhibited when reading work produced by themselves or by their group. Inhibitions seem to be more frequent when the student is required to recite or declaim a set text. This is perhaps because there is no personal investment in (the reading of) a prescribed poem.

It may be worth adding that some of the essential features of fluent speech – such as clarity of diction, phrasing, stress and rhythm, control and variation of pace – flow naturally from the reading of poetry aloud.

Compactness

One of the advantages of poems is that they offer a complete context in (usually) compact form. This is in distinction to many prose texts, which often suffer by being removed from their context. In short, a poem is a self-contained world.

The meanings conveyed in poems are usually expressed very economically. In order to retrieve these meanings and talk about them, it is necessary to expand and extend the words on the page. From a small language input one can generate a large and varied output.

A further advantage is that the vocabulary of poetry is highly associative and at the same time concentrated. This means that it can be used as the starting-point for a wide range of exercises to develop sensitivity to the webs of association which link words to each other. Such exercises can 'enhance a learner's feel for the language by giving him a sense of the weight and quality of words, and the limitations of their use in everyday speech as compared with poetic writing' (Alan Maley and Sandra Moulding, *Poem into Poem*).

Some questions

It is possible that the reader may still have some doubts about the value and practicability of using poetry as a major element in language teaching. In this section we shall be considering some of these questions.

Isn't the language of poetry too 'special'? Surely we can't offer it as a model?

– In many people's minds, 'poetry' is equivalent to a special register of English. This register is characterised by archaisms, peculiar inversions, heightened vocabulary, and so on (e.g. *hither, whence, casement, damsel, quoth, 'O Phoebus', 'nested in trees which all do seem to shake'*). But this is no longer the kind of language used by most poets. By 1920, it had very largely disappeared. There is therefore no need to

choose poetry which embodies these features. Clearly, some care needs
to be taken in selecting poems which are closer to 'normal' language.
While it is true that we would expect to find a concentration of certain
language features even in modern poetry (rhyme, rhythmic patterning,
unusual collocations, etc.), this does not inevitably occur. You might
like to decide whether the following text was originally written as prose
or poetry:

> I no longer know
> Who
> Or what
> I am.
> Or perhaps
> I know it
> Only too well.
>
> The pain swells
> To a crescendo.
> Pain that has nothing to do
> With the severed breast.
>
> I watch sister
> As she approaches
> With the syringe.
> Beautiful hands.
> Long tapering
> Fingers.
>
> And now,
> Very quietly
> I lie back
> And wait for sleep
> Thick as honey
> At the point
> Of the long, bright
> Needle.

I no longer know who or what I am. Or perhaps I know it only
too well.

The pain swells to a crescendo. Pain that has nothing to do with
the severed breast.

I watch sister as she approaches with the syringe. Beautiful
hands. Long tapering fingers.

And now, very quietly I lie back and wait for sleep, thick as
honey at the point of the long, bright needle.

(Veena Seshadri, from *I'm Not Like That*)

It has been pointed out that a poem becomes a poem by being called a poem (and by being set out typographically in a certain way). This is akin to the way in which modern painters and sculptors make 'art' (poetry) out of everyday objects (prose).

Thus modern poetry does not necessarily use special language features; what it does is to foreground ideas by putting them in a poetic frame. If this kind of poetry is chosen, the objection that the language of poetry is 'too special' disappears.

— It should be made clear that we are not suggesting that the poems be treated as models of language for immediate re-use (see earlier: Memorability). Their function is to form the centrepiece of a whole series of language activities which are more, or less, closely connected with the language of the poems themselves. That is, the poem is not treated in isolation, it is integrated with other language work.

What's the use of poetry?

— It's worth reflecting on the fact that this question could equally well be asked of any language learning activities. For instance, what is the 'use' of a set of multiple-choice questions based on any prose text? Ultimately, any activity can only be justified in terms of its results. Our contention would be that poetry should at least be given a fair trial, along with other approaches.
— This doubt may spring from the suspicion that because people rarely need to read or write poetry in life, there is little point in doing it in the classroom. This misses the point that the poem is being used not as an end in itself (a 'model') but as one part of a process. It is not that we expect the students to become 'poets', but rather to learn through the experience of grappling with words and meanings.
— It is often assumed that there should be a close correspondence between the learner's terminal aims and what he or she does in the classroom. Thus, for instance, catering staff would be exposed primarily to the English of 'the kitchen, the restaurant, the hotel' etc. Widdowson has questioned this assumption, suggesting that the learner's immediate and progressively unfolding needs may not be the same as his or her terminal objectives. Further, that their learning processes can be stimulated by a great variety of means. If this is true, there is no reason why even ESP courses should not include an element of poetry. We should not, however, wish to press this point too far.
— If we wish to define the 'use' of poetry, it is to provide a worthwhile content which has personal relevance for the learner, and to generate and sustain an integrated series of language activities.

Won't it be too difficult?

— Some poems are obviously more difficult than others. Commonsense is needed when choosing a poem for a particular group of learners. As far as possible, the level of difficulty of the poem should approximate to the level of competence of the learners. One would not, for instance, expose a group of beginners to *The Waste Land*.

— We need to remember, however, that difficulty is a relative concept. What is difficult for one is not perceived as difficult by another (the same is true of prose, of course). What we have tried to do is to offer learners access to poems through carefully chosen preparation activities and tasks to facilitate comprehension. To some extent, the teacher can select tasks of an appropriate level of difficulty for the group irrespective of the difficulty of the poem itself.

What if they don't like it?

— It is possible that some learners may have acquired a dislike for poetry from the way in which it was taught in the mother-tongue. The likelihood is that their idea of poetry is coloured by the view of poetry as a 'special language' (see the first question above). It will usually suffice to show that poetry is both interesting and 'non-poetic' by offering the student a sample of approachable poems (not necessarily modern), for example:

Vinegar

Sometimes
I feel like a priest
in a fish and chip queue
quietly thinking
as the vinegar runs through
how nice it would be
to buy supper for two.

(Roger McGough)

Poem for Roger McGough

A nun in a supermarket
Standing in the queue
Wondering what it's like
To buy groceries for two.

(Adrian Henri)

If the students need more persuading one could, for instance, collect from them a list of things they are really interested in (e.g. *football*, *TV*, *fishing*, etc.). There will certainly be poems to match some of these interests, and these could be presented as proof of the relevance of poetry to their personal concerns.

— Even though students may feel they do not like poetry, there are plenty of activities surrounding the poem which will be of interest. The aim, after all, is not to focus exclusively on the poem. It often happens that students come to enjoy poetry when they are allowed to approach the poem not head-on, but obliquely.

What if I don't like it?

The English have a proverb: 'You can lead a horse to the water but you can't make him drink'. But the French have a proverb 'l'appetit vient en mangeant' (appetite grows with eating). Not everyone will feel equally

15

comfortable with this approach but it would be a pity not to give it a try at least.

It must by now be clear that we are enthusiastic about the possibilities that poetry offers for language learning. However, our enthusiasm is tempered by realism, and we should not wish to make excessive claims. The use of poetry is for us as valid as the use of drama techniques, pictures, problem-solving, ambiguous dialogues, authentic texts, comprehension passages, sound sequences, and much else besides.

We would not suggest that this book says all there is to be said about the use of poetry in language learning – but then, could any book make such a claim? What we offer is a range/sample of suggestions and ideas which have proved their worth in practice. It is our hope that the reader will look upon them as the starting-point rather than the finishing-point of a useful and exciting exploration of language. An exploration which, fortunately, can never end. Given that it is better to travel hopefully than to arrive, we hope you will enjoy the journey.

We should be glad to hear from anyone who would like to suggest ideas that have not been included in this book, or variations on the ideas suggested here.

1 Preparing for the poem

Receptivity to a poem is usually improved if students are already tuned in to the wavelength on which it is transmitting. This chapter describes some ways in which students can be brought to think about the themes of the poems they are to read.

The preparation stage is not, as some might assume, an optional extra. Nor is it a waste of time. On the one hand, it allows students time to activate areas of their personal experience which the poem is to deal with. This creation of a mental set facilitates access to the poem. On the other, it provides rich opportunities for interaction between students. This affords valuable spin-off language-learning activity.

We shall be looking at six possible channels for approaching poems: through pictures, through the personal reactions of students, their memories etc., through recordings, through texts, through drama and role-play and through writing. This by no means exhausts the resources available for preparation but we hope it will give teachers a start in developing their own techniques.

1.1 Using pictures

For description

We can use pictures which are a direct representation of what is in the poem to be read. Here is an example:

WHAT TO DO

1 Students look at the picture on page 18, and answer, in writing, the questions which follow it:
   - What sort of dog is this?
   - What is it made of?
   - What is it looking for?
   - How will it find it?
   - Write down five adjectives which, for you, sum up the appearance of the dog.
   - How would you describe the way it is moving?
   - How would you describe its expression?
   - Where do you think this statue is?

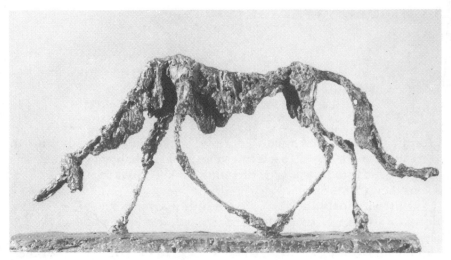

— Have you ever seen a dog like this?
— What do you think will happen when the dog arrives at its destination?
2 In pairs, students share their answers and check on how far they agree.
3 Each pair then contributes to a whole-class feedback session.
4 The poem *Giacometti's Dog* by Robert Wallace is then introduced.

Giacometti's Dog

lopes in bronze:
    scruffy
        thin. In

the Museum of Modern Art
    head
        down, neck long as sadness

lowering to hanging ears
    (he's eyeless)
        that hear

nothing, and the sausage
    muzzle
        that leads him as

surely as eyes:
    he might
        be

dead, dried webs or clots of flesh
  and fur
    on the thin, long bones – but

isn't obviously,
  is obviously
    traveling intent on his

own aim, legs
  lofting
    with a gaiety the dead aren't known

for. Going
  onward in one place,
    he doesn't so much ignore

as not recognise
  the well-
    dressed Sunday hun-

dreds who passing, pausing make
  his bronze
    road

move. Why
  do they come to admire
    him,

who wouldn't care for real dogs
  less raggy
    than he

is? Is it his tragic
  insouciance
    bugs them? or is

it that art can make us
  cherish
    anything – this command

of shaping and abutting space –
  that makes us love
    even mutts,

even the world, having
  rocks
    and the wind for comrades?

⋙→

> It's not this starved hound,
> > but Giacometti seeing
> > > him we see.
>
> We'll stand in line all day
> > to see one man
> > > love anything enough.

(Robert Wallace)

COMMENTS

There are of course many other activities which could be used to get students talking and thinking about the picture. Here are just three ideas:
- Students write their own questions about the picture (a minimum of three). They exchange these in pairs. Each student then has to answer the question they have received from their partner.
- Students write questions they would like to ask the dog. They then role-play an interview in pairs, with one student playing the dog!
- Students write down individually as many descriptive words as come to mind about the dog (e.g. *thin*, *wiry*, etc.). They compare these in pairs. They then go on to write comparisons of the form *as ... as ...* (e.g. *as thin as twigs*, *as wiry as a root* etc.). These comparisons are then discussed by the whole class, before the poem is distributed.

□ It is fairly common to come across poems with a direct reference to a picture. (For example, Brueghel's 'Death of Icarus' has inspired poems by W. H. Auden and William Carlos Williams.) One magnificent source book is *Voices in the Gallery* edited by Dannie and Joan Abse.

For suggesting a theme

We can also use pictures which suggest a theme, rather than directly representing the poem. Here is an example:

WHAT TO DO

1 Ask students to look at this picture and write down all the ideas and associations it arouses.
2 They then compare their ideas in pairs and report back to the whole class.
3 The teacher records all the ideas on the blackboard/OHP and uses them for further plenary discussion.
4 Students are then asked to write out a one-word title for the picture. These are also shared, in groups of four.
5 The poem *Commuter* is then presented.

Commuter

He lives in a house in the suburbs
He rises each morning at six.
He runs for the bus to the station,
Buys his paper and looks at the pics.

He always gets in the same carriage,
Puts his briefcase up on the rack.
Thinks miserably of his office,
And knows he can never turn back.

⋙→

He gets to his desk by nine thirty,
Wondering what he should do.
When the coffee break comes at eleven,
He knows he still hasn't a clue.

His lunch break is quite uninspiring,
He sits it out in the canteen.
It's fish and chips, mince or potatoes,
A choice that's quite literally obscene.

At five he runs back to the station,
Gets in the same carriage again,
Unfolds his evening paper,
Pulls a veil down over his brain.

(A.M.)

COMMENTS

1 Again there are plenty of other ways of getting into the theme of the pic-
  ture. Here are just three:
  – Ask students to describe a typical day in the life of this person. Com-
    pare in pairs.
  – Students are asked if this man reminds them of anyone they know.
    They jot down notes on everything they know about him, and share
    the information in pairs.
  – Students write down any words or phrases which spring immedi-
    ately to mind in connection with the picture (e.g. *tedious, vicious
    circle, drudgery, prisoner* etc.). Collect these for class discussion.
2 Once you are alert to the possibility of using pictures in this way, it is
  relatively easy to find ones which fit certain poems. It is well worthwhile starting a series of folders covering major themes (e.g. *love,
  death, work, boredom, sickness, loneliness, war, nature,* etc.) into
  which you pop any likely-looking pictures for future use. You will find
  you very rapidly develop a nose for what may be useful.

Pictures drawn or selected by students

Pictures drawn or chosen by the students themselves can provide powerful motivation, as well as focusing students' attention on a theme. Students will often say they 'can't draw'. You can reassure them by drawing
something very schematically yourself on the blackboard. Explain that
even a diagram or a map will do, provided it conveys the experience. Here
are some brief ideas:
– Students are asked to draw a picture of a close relative, e.g. father or
  mother. This could be in preparation for *Follower* by Seamus Heaney,
  Piano by D. H. Lawrence, *My Papa's Waltz* by Theodore Roethke.

22

— Students draw a picture of a childhood memory or incident. This might lead up to a poem like *It Was Long Ago* by Eleanor Farjeon, which begins 'I'll tell you, shall I, something I remember'. (See Alan Maley and Sandra Moulding, *Poem into Poem*.)
— A slightly more difficult task is to have students draw a representation of feelings aroused by, for example, war (as a preparation for *Futility* by Wilfred Owen), or separation by death from someone you were very fond of (as a preparation for Auden's poem *For Hedli Anderson* or Dylan Thomas' *In Memory of Ann Jones*).
— Rather than drawing pictures, students may be asked to collect pictures on a given theme for display in connection with a poem. For example, of birds of prey for Ted Hughes' *Hawk Roosting*.

Video

For those who have access to video, there is now a great range of material which might be used to prepare students for poems. This will be especially useful for poems with a narrative element, since the video can show stretches of action, not just frozen moments. We do not, however, have personal experience of using video in this way and cannot therefore offer specific advice. We would be pleased to hear from any readers who have used video in this way.

1.2 Personal reactions

The greatest resource we have available in the classroom is the wealth of personal experience, reminiscence and reaction stored in the students themselves. We have tried below to suggest some ways of tapping this rich reservoir.

Memories

WHAT TO DO

1 Ask students to recall their earliest memories of adults. These should not be vague but focus quite precisely on a specific memory which revealed something about 'grown-ups' they had not realised before. They write their memories up in the form of notes.
2 In pairs, they then re-tell their memories to their partners.
3 This is followed by a round-up session where the stories are noted on the blackboard/OHP in shorthand form. You, the teacher, should also contribute a memory. The following are all examples which have cropped up:

⟫→

1 Preparing for the poem

- finding mother crying – realisation that adults cry too.
- surprising widowed grandmother talking to herself while alone at home.
- being told to shut the door when sitting on the toilet – sudden realisation that others close the door.

4 Then use these memories to introduce a poem on just such an event. Here is an example of a suitable poem:

Childhood

I used to think that grown-up people chose
To have stiff backs and wrinkles round their nose,
And veins like small fat snakes on either hand,
On purpose to be grand.
Till through the banisters I watched one day
My great-aunt Etty's friend who was going away,
And how her onyx beads had become unstrung.
I saw her grope to find them as they rolled;
And then I knew that she was helplessly old,
As I was helplessly young.

(Frances Cornford)

Reactions to sensations

WHAT TO DO

1 Choose one of the five senses. In this case we will use *smell*.
2 Ask students to write down individually their favourite smell and their least favourite smell. For each smell they should then write down five words or phrases which they associate with the smell (e.g. the smell of new bread – *warm, crusty, crisp, breakfast in Paris in a pavement cafe, your hair*).
3 They then work in groups of three to exchange the information they have written down.
4 In a whole class round-up session draw up two columns on the board for *favourite/least favourite smells*, and list the items as groups report them. Is there anything in common between all the words in either column? Do any of the associated words seem odd? If so, ask for explanations.
5 Introduce the following poem:

Smells

Smells of:
> fresh fish
>> stale breath
> dry grass
>> wet dogs
> damp socks
>> moist lips
> thick smoke
>> thin grog
> dead leaves
>> live crabs
> red wine
>> green pears
> cold beds
>> hot soup
> old books
>> and . . .
>>> newspapers.

(A.D.)

COMMENTS

1 Obviously there are other ways of using sense data. For example, the feel of an object, a snatch of a song etc. can bring back a very clear memory.

2 A similar approach can be used to stimulate students' writing.

□ See also: Colours I and II (8.3, 4); Smells (8.5).

Immediate reactions

WHAT TO DO

1 Having chosen a poem, decide on a word or short phrase which sums up its theme (e.g. *cats, snow, loneliness, cruelty to old people, bureaucratic stupidity, shame* etc.).

2 Write down the word or phrase on the blackboard and give students three minutes to write down at least five words which immediately come to mind in association with it. They should not spend time thinking about this but write immediately.

3 They then work in groups of four to compare notes.

4 In the reporting back session, list the words on the board/OHP. Discuss apparently unusual items. Are there other words which now occur to students? Add these to the list.

5 Present the poem. (For *loneliness* it could be *Loneliness is . . .* (see p. 114), for *cruelty to old people* it could be *Sad Song About Greenwich Village* (see p. 85), and so on.)

COMMENTS

1 An alternative is to use a pictorial stimulus instead of a word, or even a sound (see below).
2 An additional task, once the words have been listed on the board/OHP is to ask students to sort them into two or more sets (e.g. *words we expected to find / words we did not expect to find*).

Questionnaires

WHAT TO DO

1 Devise a brief questionnaire which touches on the theme of the poem you have selected to read. Here is an example:

   1 If you were in a queue for the cinema and someone tried to push you, would you:
     a) push the person back?
     b) ask the person kindly to stop pushing?
     c) move away?
   2 You see two young boys fighting in the street. Do you:
     a) stop them?
     b) walk away?
     c) report them to their parents?
     d) call a policeman?
   3 You have left your bag on a seat at the airport for a moment, to go and buy a newspaper. On your return, the bag is on the floor, and your seat occupied by a tough-looking man. Do you:
     a) pick up the bag and move to another seat?
     b) explain it is your seat and ask him to move?
     c) call an airline official?
     d) shout at him to move?
   4 Your neighbours keep throwing junk and rubbish into your garden. Do you:
     a) throw it back again?
     b) send them a warning letter?
     c) call in the local sanitary inspector?
     d) go round to their house and tell them to stop?
(etc.)
(There is no need to continue, since these few examples should suffice. Clearly the questionnaire is about aggression and how it should be dealt with.)

2 Students answer the questionnaire individually. They then discuss, and justify, their replies in groups of three.
3 Introduce the topic of aggression and have a vote on how it should be dealt with.
4 Introduce the poem. For example, Kipling's *Danegeld*. This poem is about how easy it is for a country to give in to another's threats.

Danegeld

It is always a temptation to an armed and agile nation,
    To call upon a neighbour and to say:—
'We invaded you last night – we are quite prepared to fight,
    Unless you pay us cash to go away.'

And that is called asking for Dane-geld,
    And the people who ask it explain
That you've only to pay 'em the Dane-geld
    And then you'll get rid of the Dane!

It is always a temptation to a rich and lazy nation,
    To puff and look important and to say:—
'Though we know we should defeat you, we have not the time to
      meet you.
    We will therefore pay you cash to go away.'

And that is called paying the Dane-geld;
    But we've proved it again and again,
That if once you have paid him the Dane-geld
    You never get rid of the Dane.

It is wrong to put temptation in the path of any nation,
    For fear they should succumb and go astray;
So when you are requested to pay up or be molested,
    You will find it better policy to say:—

'We never pay any-one Dane-geld,
    No matter how trifling the cost;
For the end of that game is oppression and shame,
    And the nation that plays it is lost!'

(Rudyard Kipling)

This might later be contrasted with Stephen Spender's *My Parents Kept Me from Children who were Rough*.

☐ In this section we have only been able to expose the tip of the iceberg(?) no volcano (!) of student experience. If you are interested in other sources of ideas see Rinvolucri and Morgan, *The 'Q' Book*.

1.3 Using recordings

Interview material

WHAT TO DO

1 Choose a theme and devise a brief series of questions to ask four adults (preferably native-speakers) when you are making the recording. Here is an example:
   — Have you ever broken up with someone you loved? When?
   — Can you describe how you felt?
   — What kinds of thing did you do to get over it?
   — Did you ever meet the person again? What happened?
2 In class, play the recording to the students and ask them to record the information in note form with the help of this grid.

	When?	*Feelings?*	*Activities?*	*Meet again?*
Speaker 1				
Speaker 2				
Speaker 3				
Speaker 4				

Play the recording at least three times.
3 In pairs, students compare notes, then report back to the whole class.
4 They then complete the questionnaire about themselves, or about someone they know very well.
5 Present an appropriate poem, for example:

There are four chairs round the table

There are four chairs round the table,
Where we sit down for our tea.
But now we only set places
For Mum, for Terry and me.

We don't chatter any more
About what we did in the day.
Terry and I eat quickly,
Then we both go out to play.

Mum doesn't smile like she used to.
Often, she just sits and sighs.
Sometimes, I know from the smudges,
That while we are out she cries.

(John Foster)

COMMENTS

1 This particular example can only be done with 'consenting adults', who feel unworried when asked to discuss topics of this kind. However, the principle can be applied to almost any poem.
2 The technique offers practice in listening comprehension and involvement in discussion, so the language element in it is considerable.
3 The technique can be used in reverse order, with the poem coming first and the recording second, as a comprehension device.

Sounds

WHAT TO DO

1 Make a recording of a series of sound effects which correspond to the ones in the poem you are dealing with.
2 Ask students to listen and decide exactly what is happening. Again they will need to compare their ideas in pairs before class discussion begins.
3 Then present the poem (e.g. *Mornings* p. 102 or *In the Kitchen* p. 105).

COMMENTS

Obviously this can only be done with a limited number of poems which directly involve sound effects. For example, for *Mornings* all the noises could be recorded. However, sound recordings can also be used simply to suggest the theme of the poem. For example, for *The Listeners*, by Walter de la Mare, eerie noises and echoes of knocking could be recorded.

□ For further ideas on the use of sounds and sound sequences, see Alan Maley and Alan Duff, *Sounds Interesting* and *Sounds Intriguing*.

1.4 Reactions to texts

Titles

WHAT TO DO

1 Write the title of the poem on the board/OHP. For example: *The Responsibility* (see p. 82).
2 In pairs students speculate on what the poem with this title is likely to be about. (*Responsibility for what? Who is the person responsible? Why are they responsible?* etc.)
They should note down *several* possibilities, not just one.
3 Pairs then join to form groups of four, and combine their ideas, before reporting back to the whole class.
4 All ideas are noted on the board/OHP.
5 Present the poem *The Responsibility*. How far did any of their ideas fit?

1 Preparing for the poem

1 Clearly this is an approach which works better with some poems than others. In this book you might try it with *Bus Stop* (see p. 65), *Coat* (see p. 72) or *Island* (see p. 109).
2 With some groups it may be worth exploring the relationship of title to poem. (Quite often we can only really understand *how* to read the poem when we know the title. In other cases we only come to understand the title after we have read the poem.)

Newspaper articles

WHAT TO DO

1 Select a short newspaper article which touches on the theme of the poem you wish to work with. Here is an example:

> *Tragic Discovery*
> The body of Mrs Bridget Delaney, aged 88, was discovered when police broke into her home at Northend Road, Greenford, on Monday night.
>   The police were called after neighbours noticed she had not taken in her milk or newspapers for over a week.
>   It appears that Mrs Delaney, who lived alone, had fallen downstairs and been unable to attract the attention of her neighbours.
>   Mrs Delaney had one daughter, who is married and lives in Australia.
>
> (from the South Essex Advertiser)

2 Students read the text, then work in pairs to suggest how this tragedy could have been avoided.
3 Introduce the poem *A Sad Song About Greenwich Village* (see p. 85).

COMMENTS

1 Very often a headline will serve equally well to get students thinking along the lines of the poem.
2 Good sources for such short human interest stories are the evening and Sunday newspapers, some of which specialise in what the French call 'faits divers'.

Literary (and other) texts

WHAT TO DO

1 Choose a shortish text which relates to the theme of the poem. Here is an example:

The Iron-Age man lay slightly aslant in the peat, with the head and upper part of the body raised, resting on the bottom of the old excavation. His head lay to the north and his legs to the south. It could be seen already that he lay on his chest, with the left leg extended and the right arm and leg bent. The peat-cutters had completely exposed the head, but in doing so had damaged it to some extent. It had also been affected by the weight of the peat that had pressed down on it for centuries. In spite of all this it serves, like the head of the Tollund man, to give an impression of how this man looked on the threshold of death, many years ago. This time the effect is not one of tranquility but of pain and terror. The puckered forehead, the eyes, the mouth and the twisted posture all express it . . . There could scarcely be any doubt as to the cause of death. A long cut ran round the front of the neck practically from ear to ear, so deep that the gullet was completely severed. The wound was evidently made with several strokes by another person; the direction and appearance of the cuts showed that they could not have been self-inflicted, nor could they have been made after death. As there were no traces on the throat of cord or pressure marks that might have been caused by hanging or strangulation, the cutting of the throat was evidently the cause of death.

(P. V. Glob, from *The Bog People*)

2 Students read the text, then discuss in pairs their reactions to it. Possible prompt questions might be:
   − What is it that makes archaeological finds so interesting?
   − Have you ever seen a mummified figure?
   − What feelings do you have about this particular mummy?
3 Present the poem the *Grauballe Man* by Seamus Heaney. Here is an extract:

As if he had been paved
in tar, he lies
on a pillar of turf
and seems to weep

. . .

The head lifts,
the chin a visor
raised above the vent
of his slashed throat.

COMMENTS

1 Parallel texts, which handle the same theme or content, but in different forms, offer many opportunities for spin-offs in language work. The idea will be found in various forms in other parts of this book, e.g. Contrasts I, II and III (2.14, 15, 16).

2 Useful sources of very short literary texts are dictionaries of quotations or proverbs. Since these are sometimes organised under thematic headings (love, hope etc.), they are particularly easy of access. And, since quotations are generally chosen for their pithiness, they can be relied upon to get discussion moving before the poem is presented.

3 With advanced groups it is occasionally worth starting out with a brief extract from a review or piece of criticism of the poem. Ideally, two contrasting pieces of criticism should be presented; presenting just one view tends to prejudice students in favour of one interpretation only.

□ See also: Making choices (2.13), Contrasts I, II and III (2.14, 15, 16).

1.5 Using drama and role play

In another part of this book we explore some ways of using the text of the poem as a springboard for role play and drama. Here we are concerned with ways in which these activities can lead students up to the poem. Only one example will be given:

WHAT TO DO

1 Tell in its barest outline, the story of Daedalus and Icarus (see p. 59).

2 Divide the students into groups of three. In each group one person is to play Icarus, one Daedalus, and one a person who observed the scene from an island in the sea. Give them ten minutes to prepare a brief sketch in which they will portray the story. Each group then performs the story for another group.

3 Present the poems *Musée des Beaux Arts* and *Landscape with the Fall of Icarus* (see p. 60). What details were included in the poems, which were not included in the role-play?

COMMENTS

Drama is most readily used with poems which have either a narrative or a conflictual element.

□ Other poems in this book where this technique might be appropriate include: *I always get what I deserve, I never get what I want* (see p. 50).

1.6 Using writing

Prose writing

Another useful way of leading students to think about the theme of the poem they are to read is to get them to write about it for themselves. Here are examples of two types of writing.

WHAT TO DO
1 Individually students write down three arguments in favour of having zoos, and three arguments against zoos.
2 In groups of three, they compare their results and then decide whether, as a group, they are for or against zoos. Depending on their choice, they must then present a case for it as copy for a pamphlet to be distributed to the public.
3 Each group then presents its case to another group.
4 You then introduce the poems *The Panther* (see p. 57), and *Exile* (see p. 58).

COMMENTS
Clearly there are many other types of writing task which may be chosen to prepare for different poems. Some possibilities are: an advertisement for the 'missing persons' column to prepare for poems involving personal descriptions (e.g. *Reported Missing* by Barry Cole); newspaper headlines to accompany striking events to prepare for poems describing such events (e.g. *Tonight at Noon* by Adrian Henri); advertisements to prepare for poems involving something which might be sold or exhibited (e.g. *Grauballe Man* by Seamus Heaney); letters describing an event taking place in the poem (e.g. *Childhood* by Frances Cornford).

Writing poetry

It is often possible to reverse the usual process *reading → writing*, and to use the writing of poems as a preparation for reading them. Here are three examples where this has proved especially successful:
1 Use The clutches of the cliché (see p. 158) as preparation for e. e. cummings' poem *next to of course god america i . . .*
2 Use A sweeping nose and a running statement (see p. 153) as preparation for Edwin Morgan's poem *Spacepoem 3: Off Course* printed over the page: ⫸→

Spacepoem 3: Off Course

the golden flood   the weightless seat
the cabin song   the pitch black
the growing beard   the floating crumb
the shining rendezvous   the orbit wisecrack
the hot spacesuit   the smuggled mouth-organ
the imaginary somersault   the visionary sunrise
  the turning continents   the space debris
  the golden lifeline   the space walk
  the crawling deltas   the camera moon
  the pitch velvet   the rough sleep
  the crackling headphone   the space silence
  the turning earth   the lifeline continents
  the cabin sunrise   the hot flood
  the shining spacesuit   the growing moon
    the crackling somersault   the smuggled orbit
    the rough moon   the visionary rendezvous
    the weightless headphone   the cabin debris
    the floating lifeline   the pitch sleep
    the crawling camera   the turning silence
    the space crumb   the crackling beard
    the orbit mouth-organ   the floating song

3   Use Tangles (see 2.12) to prepare for R. D. Laing's poems from *Knots*.

Post-script
The activities described in this section can become so absorbing in themselves that the objective of preparing to read a given poem may be pushed
into the background. Try always to pace the activities so as to leave ample
time for dealing with the poem itself.

2 Working into the poem

In this chapter, we look at ways of getting students to 'do things' with poems: to find out about them by rubbing shoulders with them, by working with them, by *using* them, and not just by reading. This is what we meant in the Introduction by the *hands-on* approach. The 'Do Not Touch' notice is removed from the exhibits, and the students are allowed to 'get the feel' of what was behind the glass case.

The activities here range from those in which the student works *into* the poem – mainly through the *language* – to those in which he or she works *on* the poem, i.e. both on the *language* and on the *ideas*. There is, of course, considerable overlap between activities. In an exercise such as Missing words (2.2), for instance, the focus is on language. But in searching for the missing words in the poem the student is also exploring the underlying ideas. Likewise, in Contrasts (2.14, 15, 16), where the focus seems to be more on the ideas, the student is constantly referring back to the language.

Language and ideas are not separate – in poetry or in prose. If we have concentrated on language in many of the earlier exercises this does not mean that the content should be ignored. But simply that the approach suggested was *one* way of working into the poem. The same poem could then be used again in many of the other ways suggested in the book.

In all the activities, comprehension is involved. But 'understanding the poem' is not made the sole purpose of the exercise. An important aim is to allow the students time to *work* their way *into* the poems and discover their own interpretations. An exercise such as matching a picture to a poem, for instance, encourages the students to look closely at the text while leaving them free to respond in their own way. This is something which direct comprehension questions often fail to do.

This is why we have no 'Questions on the poem' section. There are, however, many (indirect?) questions which teachers may find useful for shaping discussion. Here is a short check-list.

- Which word in the poem struck you most? Which was the most unfamiliar/unexpected/unusual?
- Which do you think is the most important (or striking) line in the poem?
- There is a 'problem line' in the poem. Which do you think it is? Try to solve the problem with a partner.

35

— Which do you think are the 'happy' words in the poem? Make a list. Then list the 'sad' words. Compare with others. (Alternative contrasts are: long/short, concrete/abstract, loud/soft, formal/colloquial, etc.)
— There are several words in the poem relating to, for instance, *the sea, time, loneliness, the senses*. List them and compare lists with others.
— Who is speaking in the poem: the poet, someone else, or several people?
— The poem tells a story. In what order do the events occur? Are there any flashbacks or repetitions?
— Here are three titles, e.g. *Relief, Playing for Time, Lost Love*. Which do you think suits the poem best?
  Here are four pictures: which suits the poem best?
— Choose a line or phrase from the poem which could be used as a book title, the refrain of a song, a one-line message on a postcard . . . etc.
— Several comparisons are made in the poem. List as many as you can find, and discuss with a partner how accurate they are.
— Are there any lines which are ambiguous, which you do not understand, or with which you disagree?
— Are there any changes of rhythm in the poem? If so, where do they occur, and why?

2.1 Poetry or prose

WHAT TO DO

1 Divide the students into two large groups (or into pairs). Give each group or pair a text which has been written out in two ways, once as poetry, once as prose.
2 Ask them to discuss whether they think the original was poetry or prose. Encourage them to read each piece aloud.
3 Before revealing the 'answer', allow time for a group discussion, with each side defending its reasoning.

> Mr T, bareheaded, in a soiled undershirt, his hair standing out on all sides, stood on his toes, heels together, arms gracefully for the moment curled above his head. Then he whirled about, bounded into the air, and, with an entrechat perfectly achieved, completed the figure. My mother, taken by surprise where she sat in her invalid's chair, was left speechless. 'Bravo!' she cried at last, and clapped her hands. The man's wife came from the kitchen: 'What goes on here?' she said. But the show was over.
>
> (William Carlos Williams)

The languor of Youth –
How unique and quintessential it is!
How quickly, how irrecoverably, lost!
The zest, the generous affections,
The illusions, the despair,
All the traditional attributes of Youth –
All save this –
Come and go with us through life;
Again and again in riper years
We experience under a new stimulus
What we thought had been finally left behind,
The authentic impulse to action,
The renewal of power and its concentration
On a new object;
Again and again
A new truth is revealed to us
In whose light all our previous knowledge
Must be rearranged.

(Evelyn Waugh, from *Brideshead Revisited*)

COMMENTS

1 This exercise will generate quite heated discussion. Two of the main aims are:
   – to remind the students how our response to words is partly determined by the way in which they are presented, and heard or read.
   – to encourage them to look objectively at writing.
2 A variant of this idea is to give the students, working in pairs, the same prose text. They should write out the text as poetry, then compare their versions, discussing their reasons for the line-breaks.

□ See also: Contrasts I, II and III (2.14, 15, 16).

2.2 Missing words

WHAT TO DO

1 This can be done individually, in pairs, or with the students working as one large group. With large classes it is best to work in pairs.
2 Write up the text of a poem in which certain words have been left out. Each pair tries to fill in the blanks. When they have done as much as they can, they compare their versions with one or two other pairs.
3 A general round-up is held, with the teacher calling for suggestions for each missing word. As in the previous exercise these suggestions should be written up for discussion.

4 The words of the original are revealed. Here is an example:

Breaking Windows

Factory windows are always 1 ....
Somebody's 2 .... throwing bricks,
3 .... always hearing 4 .... ,
Playing ugly Yahoo 5 ....

6 .... windows are 7 .... broken.
Other 8 .... are let 9 ....
No one throws 10 .... the chapel11 ....
The bitter, 12 .... , derisive stone.

13 .... 14 .... are 15 .... 16 ....
Something or 17 .... is going 18 ....
19 .... is rotten I 20 .... in Denmark.
End of the 21 .... 22 .... song.

(Vachel Lindsay)

COMMENTS

1 It must be stressed that the purpose here is not so much to find the 'right answer' as to offer a plausible suggestion.
2 Not all poems are suitable for this exercise. One should try to choose a poem which can be fairly well grasped, even with words missing. And in deciding which words to leave out, it is important to strike a balance between the easy and the difficult, e.g. 'Something or .... is going . . . ' is fairly easy, while 'The bitter, ..., derisive stone' is more difficult. One should also try to leave out some words for which there are *clues* in the text, e.g. 'End of the .... song'.
3 It is interesting that the suggestions offered for the missing words, though different in meaning, are often very similar in *rhythm*. Even in a foreign language we can hear with 'the inward ear'.
4 The missing words: *1* broken *2* always *3* Someone's *4* children *5* tricks *6* Factory *7* always *8* windows *9* alone *10* at *11* windows *12* hard *13* Factory *14* windows *15* always *16* broken *17* other *18* wrong *19* something *20* think *21* Factory *22* window

See also: Interviews (3.7), for comparison with the poem *The Responsibility*, Just listen (4.1), Taking turns (4.11), Illustration (2.9) and Using pictures 1.1).

2.3 Alternative words

WHAT TO DO

1 Put on the board or OHP the text of a poem with three alternatives for selected words. One of the alternatives should be the word which the poet used. (See example below.)
2 In groups of four to six (or as a whole class) the students choose the word they consider most suitable in each case.

COMMENTS

1 This exercise is a variant of the 'cloze test' technique. It is particularly useful as a means of dealing with unknown, unfamiliar, or unexpected words.

   It also helps the student to work from language towards meaning and, by concentrating on *parts* of the poem, to reflect on the *whole* poem.
2 A further advantage of this technique is that it can be used on material which is already familiar to the students (or perhaps over-familiar). Approached in this way, even the best-known 'anthology pieces' can be given fresh interest, for example:

> But when the melancholy fit shall fall
>   Sudden from heaven like a (*lonely, sorrowful, weeping*) cloud,
> That fosters the (*delicate, droop-headed, dainty*) flowers all
>   And (*swathes, hides, enfolds*) the green hill in an April shroud;
> Then (*glut, ease, feed*) thy sorrow on a morning rose,
>   Or on the rainbow of the (*white capp'd, salt-sand, ever rolling*) wave,
>   Or on the wealth of globed peonies;
> Or if thy mistress some (*wild, rich, fierce, proud*) anger shows,
> Emprison her soft hand and let her rave,
> And feed deep, deep upon her peerless eyes.
>
> She dwells with Beauty — Beauty that must (*fade, die, pass, end*);
>   And Joy, whose hand is ever at his lips
> Bidding adieu; and (*aching, bitter, fleeting*) pleasure nigh,
>   Turning to Poison while the bee-mouth sips:
> Ay, in the very temple of delight
>   (*Shrouded, Veil'd, Sacred*) Melancholy has her sovran shrine,
>   Though seen of none save him whose (*eager, strenuous, sensuous*) tongue
>
> Can burst Joy's grape against his palate fine;
> His soul shall taste the (*sadness, triumph, fulness*) of her might,
>   And be among her (*airy, cloudy, precious*) trophies hung.

(Keats, from the *Ode on Melancholy*)

2.4 Missing lines

WHAT TO DO

1 The class works as a single large group. A short poem, in which two or three lines are missing, is written up or dictated.
2 The students call out their suggestions for the missing lines. These are written up on the board or noted down by a student who has agreed to act as 'secretary'.
3 There is now a brief discussion on which suggestions the students find most/least acceptable, which are questionable from the point of view of language, which do not fit the sense of the poem, etc.
4 The original lines are now given, and the poem is read out in its complete form.

Here is an example:

In This City

In this city, perhaps a street.
In this street, perhaps a house.
1 .... , ...
.... ,
And in this room a woman sitting,
Sitting in the darkness, sitting and crying
For someone who *2* ....
....
And who has just switched off the light
3 ....

(Alan Brownjohn)

COMMENTS

1 The exercise should not be made too difficult. The purpose is to encourage intelligent guesses, not to baffle. Short poems, particularly those which contain repetition, are likely to be most suitable.
2 *Writing up* the students' suggestions as they come helps to provide a reference point for later discussion. For instance, were there any clues in the text which were missed? (Here, the line 'who *has* just *switched off* the light' is a pointer to the tense of the previous line 'who *has* just *gone* through the door').
3 The poem is not 'finished' when the exercise is done. The same poem can be approached from a different angle in other activities.
4 The missing lines:
   1 In this house, perhaps a room.
   2 (For someone who) has just gone through the door.
   3 Forgetting she was there.

☐ See also: Using pictures (1.1), Themes (3.5, 6), Interviews (3.7), Word portraits (3.9), That's life (5.2).

2.5 Jumbled lines

WHAT TO DO

1 Read out or write on the board the text of a poem in which the lines are given out of order. (Maximum length: twelve lines.)
2 The students, working in pairs, try to put the lines back into their original order. (Time limit: six minutes.)
3 Round-up session: the class as a whole builds up the poem, line-by-line. Any disagreements should be noted. Finally, the original version is read out.

Here is an example:

Dream Deferred

Like a heavy load
Or crust and sugar over –
Does it dry up
Like a syrupy sweet?
Or does it explode?
And then run?
Maybe it just sags
Or fester like a sore –
Like a raisin in the sun?
Does it stink like rotten meat?

(Langston Hughes)

(NB The first line of the poem is: 'What happens to a dream deferred?')

COMMENTS

Short poems are most suitable, particularly those with lines which can be variously combined.

☐ This poem could also be used in the following exercises: Using pictures (1.1), Newspaper articles (1.4), Dramatisation/role play (3.8), When I'm old (5.5).

41

2.6 Fractured phrases

1   Students work in groups of eight. Each group is given slips of paper on which are written phrases. The phrases are derived from a poem which has been broken up. For example:

There was just	at the flute end
The hands gripped hard	that never cared less.
At noon	the elbows waited
a panting lizard	of a particular road
Watching the curve	as if something
It was looking	at something
	its elbows tense
for little selves	waited for history
a continent	in the desert
under a sky	an important scene
might happen	of consequences
farther off	Ready for a change
acted in stone	then people could see.
without much on it	
in the desert	

2   Each group then attempts to form as many complete sentences as possible. (The same phrase may be used in more than one sentence.)
3   Groups then exchange their lists of sentences and attempt to put the sentences in order, so as to form a poem. At this point they may be told that the title of the poem is *At the Bomb Testing Site*. They are also told it has three stanzas, each of four lines.
4   They can then revise their poems before returning them to the groups from which they received the original sentences.
5   The original poem is then presented.

At the Bomb Testing Site

At noon in the desert a panting lizard
waited for history, its elbows tense,
watching the curve of a particular road
as if something might happen.

It was looking at something farther off
than people could see, an important scene
acted in stone for little selves
at the flute end of consequences.

There was just a continent without much on it
under a sky that never cared less.
Ready for a change, the elbows waited.
The hands gripped hard on the desert.

(William Stafford)

COMMENTS

The sentence-building aspect of this exercise is in itself valuable for trying out sentences for acceptability. The poem-making leads to useful inter-action centring on the meaning.

□ This is a similar exercise to Tangles (2.12) which starts from words and Jumbled lines (2.5) which re-orders the lines of a poem.

2.7 Building up from memory

WHAT TO DO

1 Read aloud or play a recording of a poem you consider suitable for *listening* to.
2 After the first reading, ask the class to call out any words or fragments of the poem they can remember. Note these on the board (or ask one of the students to do this). Allow for disagreement and uncertainty (e.g. 'I think there was something about "wind-blinded"').
3 Read the poem once again. This time, working in pairs, the students write down as much as they can remember together of the poem. When they have finished, they join another pair and help each other to fill in the gaps.
4 After about five minutes, call for a round-up session in which the whole class tries to build up the poem line-by-line.
5 If you wish, move on to a short discussion of the poem. A useful way of starting is to ask: 'Which lines or phrases did you find hardest to *remember*? In many cases these will also turn out to be the passages the student found hardest to understand.
   Here is an example:

Snowdrops

Yesterday I walked
through the churchyard
and noticed
for the first time
the snowdrops
on the graves.

»→

They must
have been there
for days
but I
was wind-blinded,
huddled into myself,
so anxious
to retain
my solitary
identity
that nothing
could touch me,
that I
could touch nothing.

(Patricia Pogson)

COMMENTS

1 Generally, the poems most suitable for this exercise are either those with strong rhythm and rhyme, or those with a clear narrative line (D. H. Lawrence's *Snake*, for instance).

2 This can be seen as an oblique approach to comprehension. The focus is on remembering rather than understanding. Instead of giving the students the poem and asking 'What does it mean?' (as is so often done!), we ask them simply to piece it together from memory. By the time they have done this, they are already *familiar* with the poem, and so better able to talk about it, or use it in some of the ways described in this book.

3 Students have at times remarked that they 'do not like hearing poetry read aloud'. One of the commonest objections is: 'I find it much easier to concentrate when I can *read* the text'. This resistance is quite understandable, particularly in a foreign language. In addition, the teacher may feel apprehensive about reading aloud. If there is resistance in the class, we suggest you first try an exercise such as Fractured phrases (2.6): this will help to familiarise the students with the poem through *speaking* rather than *listening*. But the process is the same: building up the poem fragment by fragment.

□ See also: Just listen and other exercises in Speaking poetry (chapter 4), Illustration (2.9), Editor's choice (3.1).

2.8 Visualisation

For this exercise, visual material such as a video-tape or filmstrip is needed. Such material is not yet widely available, and what exists may well be beyond the means of the average school or language centre. But recent developments, particularly in video material, encourage us to think that 'poetry through pictures' will soon be accessible to all. (See Earl Stevick, *Images and Options*.)

Below is a brief description of how one might work with an already existing video-tape: *The Highwayman*, by Alfred Noyes (see p. 91).

WHAT TO DO

1 Play the tape right through to the students, without a break. (It is, of course, a matter of personal choice whether or not a brief introduction should be given. In this case, however, we feel that the teacher should resist the temptation to summarise the story and explain unfamiliar words.)
2 After viewing the tape, the students work in pairs. Together, they try to recall as accurately as possible the *sequence* of the images. Any fragments of the poem they can remember should be noted down. Allow five to ten minutes for this.
3 When ready, each pair compares notes with another pair. Any 'gaps' in the story should be noted.
4 Before playing the tape again, ask the students: a) to mention any incidents that were not clear to them, b) to recall any fragments of the poem.
5 At this stage, you will probably want to proceed in your own way. We therefore suggest only two of the many possibilities:
   – The students remain in pairs. Each pair looks at a copy of the text. They go through it together, marking the points to which they think the images on the tape correspond. While they are doing this, the teacher circulates to answer any questions (though the students should be encouraged not to ask yet for explanations). It helps to set a strict time-limit for the reading – ten to twelve minutes.

   The tape is now played again. Each pair notes the points in the text where the images change.

   When the tape is finished, the students go rapidly through the text again, marking *only* those passages which they feel were not conveyed visually, i.e. there was no image to match the words. They then compare notes in groups of four.
   – The text is divided up. The students work in pairs, each pair dealing with one verse. For example:

⟫→

45

Nearer he came and nearer! Her face was like a light!
Her eyes grew wide for a moment; she drew one last
deep breath,
Then her finger moved in the moonlight,
Her musket shattered the moonlight,
Shattered her breast in the moonlight and warned him –
with her death.

The students are told to look with particular care at the images which correspond to their passage. The tape is then played again.

After the second viewing, each pair exchanges verses with another. Each tries to describe as accurately as possible the images that went with the text they have now been given. The other pair listens, and then points out what they may not have noticed.

COMMENTS

1   It is worth recalling here that one of the aims of this book is to suggest ways in which poetry can be used as language learning material – as prose already is. Discussion, therefore, is important. And discussion need not always mean *analysing* the poem.
2   In this exercise we have tried to show how the *visual* presentation of a poem can make it possible for the students to discuss ideas which would not normally emerge from a cold reading of the text. It is not that the text is ignored, for the students will be constantly referring to the *words* in discussing the images. It is merely that the emphasis is not exclusively on the text. The text is the starting-point, not the end-point.
3   Even without the aid of video, students can be encouraged to visualise poems. Some suggestions can be found in Using pictures (1.1) and also in chapter 3).
4   A further alternative is to ask the students to write the filmscript for videoing a poem. This involves them in deciding which shots they will need for which lines in the poem. They should write out the script in two columns:

Text	*Shots*
In this city, perhaps a street	Zoom in on city street scene – deserted
In this street, perhaps a house (etc.)	Zoom in to one house in the street (etc.)

If equipment and time allow, they may be asked to make the video.

2.9 Illustration

WHAT TO DO

1 The students work in groups of three. Each group looks at three or four poems – the same poems for all – and a selection of pictures. The pictures need not be the same.
2 Each group selects a picture that could be used as an illustration for one of their poems.
3 (Optional) When they have matched one picture with a poem, they may exchange pictures with other groups to make a second match.
4 If the class is large, one group joins another. If it is small, a round-up session is held. The groups now show the picture(s) they have chosen, and explain how they illustrate the poems.

COMMENTS

1 The length of the poem does not matter. This exercise can be done with any poem, long or short. Short poems, however, are often difficult to discuss. So this is one way of opening them out.
2 The exercises can be made more explicit by asking the students to decide on the *context* of the poem and the illustration. 'Where do they appear – in a book, a magazine, a newspaper, on a piece of needlework, a mural, a television screen?' etc. And could the picture be a *criticism* of the poem?
□ See also: Using pictures (1.1), Personal reactions (1.2), Editor's choice (3.1), Criticism (2.18), Word portraits (3.9), Visualisation (2.8).

2.10 One at a time

WHAT TO DO

1 Choose a fairly short poem (e.g. In This City, see p. 40). Write the first line only on the blackboard or OHP:

> In this city, perhaps a street.

2 Ask students to note down
   a) the visual impression they get from this line.
   b) any questions which occur to them (e.g. Which city? Why does he say 'perhaps'? What will he say next? etc.).
They then compare their impressions and questions in pairs. These can then be shared in full class discussion.
3 Add the second line:

> In this city, perhaps a street.
> In this street, perhaps a house.

and follow the same procedure (e.g. What kind of house? I wonder if the next line will start 'In this house . . . '? etc.).

4 Add line 3:

> In this city, perhaps a street.
> In this street, perhaps a house.
> In this house, perhaps a room.

Again follow the same procedure (e.g. I wonder what will be in the room? Will there be any people in this poem? Is it about ghosts? etc.).

5 Add line 4:

> In this city, perhaps a street.
> In this street, perhaps a house.
> In this house, perhaps a room.
> And in this room a woman sitting,

Follow the same procedure (e.g. What kind of woman? Why doesn't he use 'perhaps' this time? I wonder how old she is. Why is she sitting there? etc.).

6 Add line 5:

> In this city, perhaps a street.
> In this street, perhaps a house.
> In this house, perhaps a room.
> And in this room a woman sitting,
> Sitting in the darkness, sitting and crying

Follow the same procedure (e.g. Why is she in darkness: is it a power failure? Why is she crying? etc.).

7 Continue to the final line.

8 Round off with a discussion of the picture students now have of the incident. Ask them to write a short paragraph giving their own interpretation of the poem. For example:

> This old lady lives with her son and daughter-in-law in a small flat in the suburbs of London. They are very busy people and they find it a nuisance to have her around all the time, so she tries to keep out of their way as much as possible. One day her son came into the room to look for something. She was sitting quietly in the corner knitting, so he didn't notice her. As he went out, he switched off the light. She burst into tears.

COMMENTS

1 This progressive unveiling of the poem obliges the students to focus sharply on every bit of meaning and to visualise, speculate and anticipate. The differences in mental imagery from student to student are revealing, and show how important individual interpretation is in the

comprehension of the poem.
2   It also offers scope for a progressive revision of opinion as new information is released.
3   One useful variation on this activity is to begin by writing up the *last* line and work backwards towards the beginning. You might try this with *Coat* (see p. 72).

□   See also: Line-by-line unfolding (2.11).

2.11 Line-by-line unfolding

WHAT TO DO
1   Give the students the title and first line of a short poem. Ask them to suggest what the second line might be.
2   When all suggestions have been heard, write up the second line, and ask for the third . . . and so on, till the end of the poem.

Here is an example:

'If I might be an ox'

If I might be an ox,
An ox, a beautiful ox,
Beautiful but stubborn:
The merchant would buy me,
Would buy me and slaughter me,
Would spread my skin,
Would bring me to the market,
The coarse woman would bargain for me,
The beautiful girl would buy me.
She would crush perfumes for me,
I would spend the night rolled up round her,
I would spend the afternoon rolled up round her.
Her husband would say: 'It is a dead skin.'
But I would have her love.

(Anon; a song of the Galla tribe in Ethiopia, translator unknown)

COMMENTS
1   Several variants of this approach are possible. Here are a few:
    –   Choose a poem with strong end rhymes, e.g. *break, light, takes, flight*. Write up only the rhyming words at the end of each line. In pairs, the students devise lines to end with these rhymes.
    –   Give one line in full, and only the last word of the following line. The students work through the poem, filling in each second line.

— Give the first and last words of each line.
— Give the full text, leaving out only the end rhyme.

□ See also: Rhyme and reason (6.14), Word webs (6.1) and Fractured phrases (2.6). Bouts rimés (6.15).

2.12 Tangles (Jumbled words)

WHAT TO DO

1 Take a short, not too complex poem, and break it up into its component words. Write these out, in any order, e.g.

because	since	therefore	deserve
not	do/don't	can/can't	want
I	you	shall	must
is	have	what	never
get	it	only	

(All these words are taken from the two poems below, by R. D. Laing.)
2 Working in pairs, the students combine the words to make as many meaningful sentences as they can. Two changes are allowed: verbs, in the present tense, can take the -s ending (3rd person), and the *n't* contraction (e.g. isn't).
3 After ten minutes, the pairs exchange notes, marking any sentences which are *exactly* the same as those of another pair. Here are a few typical sentences:
I don't want what you do.
I want you because I don't deserve you.
You do what I can't, what you can't I do.
I don't get it.
4 Round-up session: each pair calls out one or two formulations which they have *not* heard from other pairs. (Allow time for discussion of borderline cases, e.g. 'I have, therefore you want'.)
5 Now let the class read the two poems below. Allow time for discussion and for comparison with their own word combinations.

> *I*
>
> I never got what I wanted
> I always got what I did not want.
> What I want
>   I shall not get.
>
> *Therefore*, to get it
>   I must not want it
> *since* I get only what I don't want

what I want, I can't get
what I get, I don't want

I can't get it
  because I want it

I get it
  because I don't want it

I want what I can't get
  because
what I can't get is what I want

I don't want what I can get
  because
what I can get *is* what I don't want

I never get what I want
I never want what I get.

II

I get what I deserve
I deserve what I get
I have it,
    therefore I deserve it.

I deserve it
  because I have it.

You have not got it
  therefore you do not deserve it

You do not deserve it
  because you have not got it

You have not got it
  because you do not deserve it

You do not deserve it
therefore you have not got it.

(R. D. Laing, *Knots*)

COMMENTS

1 The most suitable poems are those which can be 'broken up' without being destroyed. Here is another example which works very well.

> I am dead because I lack desire;
> I lack desire because I think I possess;
> I think I possess because I do not try to give.

⟫→

> In trying to give, you see that you have nothing;
> Seeing you have nothing, you try to give of yourself;
> Trying to give of yourself, you see that you are nothing;
> Seeing that you are nothing, you desire to become;
> In desiring to become, you begin to live.

> (John Heilpern, from *The Conference of the Birds*)

Fragments from longer poems (e.g. T. S. Eliot's *Four Quartets*) could also be used.

2   One way to prepare for this is to select an array of words which will yield a rich selection of sentences. For example:

do	be	question	you	not
tell/told	is	want	what	know
answer	need	if	to	the
I	ask/asked			

   – To be told is not to know.
   – Why ask the question, if you know the answer?
   – Do not question the answer/Do not answer the question.
   – What you need to know is not what I tell you.
   – To want is to need, to be needed is to be wanted.
   – Why (do you) ask if you do not want to know?
   – Why ask if you know?
   – What you want, I do not know.
   – What you know, I do not want.
   – I do not want to know what I am told.
   – I do not want to be told what I know.
   – I do not want to answer the question.
   – Do you know what you want?
   – The answer is not to be.
   – Question not the need.

Students may then go on to write their own poem, by selecting and ordering sentences they have constructed.

☐ See also: Titles (1.4), Taking turns (4.11), What I love about . . . (5.6), Word webs (6.1), Computer poems (7.9), Fractured phrases (2.6), A little goes a long way (8.1).

2.13 Making choices (Begging your pardon, Lord Tennyson)

WHAT TO DO

1   Offer three versions of a poem. For example:

a) *The Eagle*

He grips the rock with crooked hands,
Near to the sun in distant lands.
Surrounded by the sky he stands.

The crumpled sea beneath him froths.
He looks out from the mountain tops.
And like a deadly stone, he drops.

b) *The Eagle*

He grasps the cliff with ruthless claws.
Close to the sun he writes his laws.
Encircled by the heavens, he soars.

The furrowed deep below him crawls.
He scans the world from his mountain halls.
Then, like a judgement day, he falls.

c) *The Eagle*

He clasps the crag with crooked hands,
Close to the sun in lonely lands,
Ring'd with the azure world, he stands.

The wrinkled sea beneath him crawls;
He watches from his mountain walls,
And like a thunderbolt he falls.

2 Explain that these are three versions of the same poem found among the papers of a poet after his death. Individually, each student is to decide which of the versions is the one finally chosen by the poet, and why.
3 Students then work in pairs to discuss and justify their choices. This is then rounded off with class discussion.

COMMENT

1 Students usually only meet with finished products. Here we attempt to introduce them to the processes which lead to these products. Essentially the poet is confronted by choices at every point. Why this word rather than that? (Is it because it fits the rhythmic pattern or the rhyme scheme better? Is it because it conveys a sharper image? Or because it chimes with a pattern of alliteration or assonance? Or . . . ?)
2 In this way students themselves are brought to consider whether: 'He clasps the crag with crooked hands' is more satisfying or effective than 'He grasps the cliff with ruthless claws', and if so, why. All too often

they are asked to evaluate lines or poems in isolation. By offering the possibility of comparison, this activity makes the process both more concrete and more realistic. Teachers who feel the exercise may be too difficult could first try using the suggestions in Translations (2.20).

3 A possible variation is to offer three versions which, between them, contain all the lines of the final version. They then 'quarry' the three versions to construct what they feel to be a finished product.

☐ For further examples, see *The Collected Poems of D. H. Lawrence* and *The Poems of William Blake*. Both these editions give variants of lines and passages which were later rejected by the poets.

2.14 Contrasts I

WHAT TO DO

1 Choose two poems which parallel each other in some way (in theme, form, vocabulary etc.).
2 Ask students to read the two poems very carefully. Each student is to note down three similarities between them, and three differences.
3 In pairs, students compare their ideas and report back in plenary class discussion.

Here is an example:

When you are old

When you are old and grey and full of sleep
And nodding by the fire, take down this book,
And slowly read, and dream of the soft look
Your eyes had once, and of their shadows deep.

How many loved your moments of glad grace,
And loved your beauty with love false or true;
But one man loved the pilgrim soul in you,
And loved the sorrows of your changing face.

And bending down beside the glowing bars
Murmur, a little sadly, how love fled
And paced upon the mountains overhead
And hid his face amid a crowd of stars.

(W. B. Yeats)

When I am old

When I am old and grey
And full of death,
Caress me still,
And with your breath
Assure me that I live.

Despite all proof of imminent collapse
Contrive to bring relief,
Through your belief
In permanence of a kind, perhaps.

When winter's light pales down
To dark and cold and void,
Let us be gay in living
What we can't avoid.

Let death be sure
We will not let him gloat,
But rather stuff his message
Down his throat!

(A.M.)

COMMENTS

1 Clearly poems will resemble, and differ from, each other in different
ways. It may be worth explaining these at the plenary discussion stage
(though not before, otherwise students will be conditioned to look at
the poems in pre-determined ways). Here are some possible avenues of
approach to the poems given above:
   – Vocabulary – are there any identical words? Any synonyms? Any
     words belonging to the same lexical family?
   – Structures – are there any resemblances in the grammatical patterns
     or forms used? (e.g. same tense, use of rhetorical questions, use of
     imperative etc.)
   – Form – do the poems have the same number of verses? Do the verses
     have the same number of lines? Do the lines have the same number
     of syllables, the same rhythm? Is the rhyme scheme the same?
   – Mood – which words from those given best describe the mood of
     each poem? (*resigned, rueful, regretful, angry, mournful, defiant,
     dejected, violent, soulful, disappointed* etc.)
   – Message – do the poems have an identical message?
   – Personae – Who is speaking in each poem? Who to?
2 The process of comparison seems to help students notice things they
might miss if they were presented with one poem alone. With close and

repeated readings, the similarities are reinforced, and the differences strike sparks of recognition, which enrich the understanding of both poems.

☐ There are a number of sources of paired poems for comparison. See in particular *Poem into Poem*, A. Maley and S. Moulding; *Double Take*, ed. F. Bolt.

2.15 Contrasts II

WHAT TO DO

1 Ask the class as a whole to think of *specific* animals in city zoos (e.g. *elephant, polar bear, giraffe, monkey, cobra, mountain goat*). For each animal they should note: (a) What it would most *miss* or *want*, (b) What it would most *dislike* about life in the zoo. (Vague words such as *freedom* should be qualified, e.g. 'The gazelle would miss being able to run across the savannah'.)

2 The students work in pairs. Each pair looks at the poems *Exile* and *The Panther*.

3 After silent reading, they make a note of any striking similarities or differences between the two poems. While they are doing this, write up on the board a few guidelines for discussion, for example:
   – Is there anything in your notes (from 1) which is echoed in the poems?
   – In the poem *Exile*, what animal is speaking? What words help you to decide?
   – If you were to photograph the animal in each poem, what would the photograph show?
   – Choose a line (or fragment) from each poem which you could use as a caption for your photograph.
   – Note any words or phrases from either poem which you do not fully understand.
   – Compare the endings of the two poems: 'Only at dusk I dare to dream . . . plotting my return', and 'Only from time to time . . . a picture enters . . . and ceases to be'. In what ways are they similar, in what ways different?

4 Each pair now exchanges notes with at least two other pairs. Points of divergence or disagreement should be recorded.

5 (Optional) Now proceed to one of the exercises which involve close study of a text, e.g. Paraphrase (2.17) or Everyday things (3.2, 3, 4).

COMMENTS

1 In the Introduction, we have said that one of the strongest reasons for using poetry in foreign language teaching is that it provides material which is *open to interpretation*, and hence discussion. But it is not always easy to 'discuss' a poem when one is faced with a text and a set of questions on it. The discussion tends to be limited to answering the questions.

   The great value of *contrast* is that it provides a second point of reference – a 'sounding-board', if you like – and that it encourages the students to look for connections rather than merely answer questions.

2 The contrast, however, should not be forced. This is why it is advisable to set a time-limit to the discussion. This is also why we have suggested using this exercise as a preparation for activities which require close study of a text.

3 It is important for the students to think around the theme (of captivity) before coming to the poems. Their *notes* provide a valuable starting-point for discussion.

□ See also: Reactions to texts (1.4), Illustration (2.9), Themes (3.5, 6), In character (4.9), I wish I . . . (5.4).

The Panther

In the Jardin des Plantes, Paris

Year after year the bars go pacing past,
till in the end his very brain is blind.
With eyes wide open, all he sees at last
is bars, bars, bars, and emptiness behind.

And as he pads his cage with supple grace,
tracing his tiny circle, round and round,
a force goes turning, dancing round a place
in which a mighty will stands dumb and bound.

Sometimes the curtain briefly moves away.
An image enters, flickers past the eyes,
speeds through the waiting body, finds its way
straight to the heart; and dies.

(Rainer Maria Rilke, translated by Michael Swan)

The Jardin des Plantes is a small park and botanical garden, which includes a zoo, in the centre of Paris.

Exile

My shade is striped
My air is barred
(As it was before;
Only here the bars
Do not bend with the wind.)

My breath is short
My claws are blunt
With long pacing on stone ground.
All day I smell
Zebra . . . gazelle . . .
But I am full of easy meat
I have no appetite.

Only at dusk –
When the monkeys mock from stone trees
And the buck (soft noses sniffing the air
For the scent they no longer fear)
Come down to the mudless pool to drink –
Only at dusk I dare to dream
Eyes half-closed, bending the bars
Against the sun
And plotting my return.

(A.D.)

2.16 Contrasts III

WHAT TO DO

1 The students work in groups of three. Each group looks at the prose text on 'Daedalus and Icarus' (see page 59).
2 Ask them to note down, very briefly, the main details shown or mentioned in each, e.g. *wax, wings, sun, sea, field, farmer, plough*, etc.
3 Each group now reads the poems in this chapter by Auden and William Carlos Williams (*Musée des Beaux Arts* and *The Fall of Icarus*) and the extract from *Oedipus* by Ted Hughes. For each detail on their lists, they should try to find a reference in one of the poems.
4 They now draw up two lists: points of *difference* and points of *similarity*. For instance, *similarity*: 'a splash quite unnoticed' and 'everything turns away quite leisurely from the disaster'; *difference* – 'the expensive delicate ship that must have seen something amazing' and 'insignificantly off the coast . . . '.

5 If the class is large, ask each group to compare notes with two other groups; if small, ask each group to read out its lists.

COMMENTS

1 If it is difficult to reproduce the illustration, for example with an OHP, allow each group to study the page for two minutes, while the others are working on the prose text.
2 The reason for asking the students at first to focus only on the physical details is to give them a clear starting-point. At this stage they do not need to interpret, merely to note. The interpretation will follow naturally once they start looking for similarities and differences.
3 Two points worth bearing in mind are:
   – The importance of *writing down* the relevant lines or words (in stages 3 and 4). This helps them to get to know the poems and also to discover which groups of words belong together in spite of line-breaks, e.g. 'the whole pageantry/of the year/was awake . . . '
   – The value of *open contrast*, i.e. the groups are free to choose their own words or phrases for comparison – several different matchings are possible.

□ See also: Reactions to texts (1.4), Building up from memory (2.7), Themes (3.5, 6), Dramatisation (3.8), Keywords (8.10, 11).

The Legend of Daedalus and Icarus
(Daedalus, a master-craftsman, and his son Icarus were imprisoned on the island of Crete. Their prison was the maze of the Minotaur – a terrible beast, half-man, half-bull. Thanks to the skill of Daedalus, they managed to escape from the maze. But there was only one way they could get away from the island – by flying over the sea. Out of birds' feathers, wood and wax, Daedalus made the wings . . .)

> When the wings were ready, they strapped them to their arms. Before they took to the air, Daedalus warned his son, once again: 'Do not fly too high. The sun will melt the wax on your wings.'
> They kissed and embraced. Daedalus launched himself into the air, Icarus following close behind. They climbed higher, and the wings held. Daedalus showed his son how to keep his direction, how to glide and turn, and for a while Icarus kept close.
> From the land, now far below them, men looked up in amazement. Farmers stopped their ploughing, shepherds turned from their sheep. And as the two winged men flew out over the sea, the fishermen looked up from their boats, not believing what they saw. Sailors ran to the sides of their ships.
> Then Icarus, confident now, flew past his father and higher and higher . . . Daedalus tried to shout, but the strain of beating his wings made his voice faint. And soon the feathers began to

c

drop, one by one, from Icarus' wings. The harder he beat his
arms, the faster the feathers fell. Soon Icarus, too, was falling –
plunging – towards the sea. As he fell, he shouted out his
father's name. And his father shouted back: 'Icarus. Where are
you? Where? . . . ' He did not hear the faint splash. Not even a
ripple marked the place where Icarus had fallen.

(Unknown)

Musée des Beaux Arts

About suffering they were never wrong,
The Old Masters: how well they understood
Its human position; how it takes place
While someone else is eating or opening a window or just
     walking dully along;
How, when the aged are reverently, passionately waiting
For the miraculous birth, there always must be
Children who do not specially want it to happen, skating
On a pond at the edge of the wood:
They never forgot
That even the dreadful martyrdom must run its course
Anyhow in a corner, some untidy spot
Where the dogs go on with their doggy life and the torturer's
     horse
Scratches its innocent behind on a tree.

In Brueghel's *Icarus*, for instance: how everything turns away
Quite leisurely from the disaster; the ploughman may
Have heard the splash, the forsaken cry.
But for him it was not an important failure; the sun shone
As it had to on the white legs disappearing into the green
Water; and the expensive delicate ship that must have seen
Something amazing, a boy falling out of the sky,
Had somewhere to get to and sailed calmly on.

(W. H. Auden)

Landscape with the Fall of Icarus

According to Brueghel
when Icarus fell
it was spring

a farmer was ploughing
his field
the whole pageantry

of the year was
awake tingling
near

the edge of the sea
concerned
with itself

sweating in the sun
that melted
the wings' wax

insignificantly
off the coast
there was

a splash quite unnoticed
that was
Icarus drowning.

(William Carlos Williams)

foolish Icarus   he thought he could fly
it was a dream
tried to crawl   across the stars
loaded with his crazy dream   his crazy paraphernalia
the wings the wax and the feathers
up and up and up
saw eagles beneath him   saw his enormous shadow on the
    clouds beneath him
met the sun face to face
fell

his father Daedalus was wiser   he flew lower
he kept under clouds   in the shadow of the clouds
the same crazy equipment   but the dream different
till Icarus dropped past him   out of the belly of a cloud
past him
down
through emptiness
a cry   dwindling
a splash

tiny in the middle of the vast sea.

(Seneca, from *Oedipus*, translated by Ted Hughes)

2.17 Paraphrase

WHAT TO DO

1 The students work in groups of three. Each group looks at two or three prose paraphrases or summaries of a poem, and the text of the poem.
2 They should read each paraphrase carefully and discuss which they think is the closest description of the poem.
3 After eight to ten minutes, the groups break up – even though they may not have reached agreement. New groups of two to four are now formed, and the discussion continues.
4 A short round-up session is held to pool the groups' reactions.

COMMENTS

1 It is essential that each summary be a *credible* explanation of the poem, inaccurate only in certain details. The students should be encouraged to check such paraphrase line-by-line against the poem.
2 Like the previous three exercises (Contrasts I, II and III) this is an excellent way of helping students to 'work their way into' a poem without having to answer comprehension questions on it.

☐ See also: Using pictures (1.1), Word portraits (3.9), Editor's choice (3.1), Love/hate (5.6), and Using writing (1.6) comments.

Here is an example of material which could be used for this activity.

> *Pity*
>
> 'At the mineral fair'
> he said
> 'there was this dealer
> he had an Indian skull
> you know them Indian skulls.
> In the front
> there was a bullet hole
> and at the back of the skull
> a flattened musket ball
> embedded, like.
> I've always wanted one of them things.
> Look good in the living-room –
> sort of conversation-piece.
> But I could just hear the wife:
> "Get that horrible thing out of here."
> Pity, though.'
>
> (Michael Swan)

Which of the following do you think best reflects the meaning of the poem?

a) The poem is a fragment of conversation overheard. The poet does not comment directly on what he hears. But he suggests through the title that the speaker and his wife are equally insensitive, in different ways. *He* sees the skull as merely an interesting decoration, something to talk about to guests. *She* (he is sure) will see it as a disgusting object. What unites them is that neither feels any pity for the man who died.

b) This is a poem about an unhappy marriage. Although the poet does not comment directly, he indicates through the title that it is unfortunate that such a sensitive man should be married to such an insensitive woman. The speaker has a genuine interest in history, he loves old things, and he has a good eye for detail. He is also fond of company. It is a pity that his wife shares none of these interests.

c) The poem is a gentle satire on ordinary people who cannot find the right language to express their feelings. The poet deliberately uses colloquial speech to show how easily misunderstandings can arise when people cannot find the words to say what they mean. The speaker is a simple man, who tends to repeat himself. The 'pity' of it is that he can't explain to his wife – as he can to his friend – why he wants to take the skull home.

2.18 Criticism

WHAT TO DO

1 The students work in groups of three. Each group works on the same poem or poems.
2 Allow about five minutes for silent reading. While the students are reading, write up on the board/OHP a selection of words such as:

striking	awkward	unexpected	ambiguous
powerful	weak	odd	unclear
stiff	clever	impersonal	unfinished
cruel	honest	sentimental	true

3 The groups now look for lines or phrases in the poem(s) to which any of these words *might* apply. They need not use all the words.
4 After discussion, they compare notes with other groups.

COMMENTS

1 Particularly suitable for advanced students.
2 The exercise requires great *precision* in the use of language. The students should be able to give reasons for matching a word against a particular phrase. In the discussion it will emerge that many different

matchings are possible. And also that the stimulus words can refer to different aspects of the poem, e.g. *odd* might refer to *rhythm*, *choice of words*, *comparison*, *image*, *statement* or *idea*.

3 The stimulus words can, of course, be changed. For more ideas, see the introduction to this chapter.

4 Last, but certainly not least: *criticism* is not only negative, it also includes *appreciation* (and of course 'understanding').

□ See also: Illustration (2.9), Paraphrase (2.17), Editor's choice (3.1), Contrasts (2.14, 15, 16), In character (4.9), Keywords (8.10, 11).

Here is an example:

One Cigarette

No smoke without you, my fire
After you left,
your cigarette glowed on in my ashtray
and sent up a long thread of such quiet grey
I smiled to wonder who would believe its signal
of so much love. One cigarette
in the non-smoker's tray.
As the last spiral
trembles up, a sudden draught
blows it winding into my face.
Is it smell, is it taste?
You are here again, and I am drunk on your tobacco lips.
Out with the light.
Let the smoke lie back in the dark
Till I hear the very ash
sigh down among the flowers of brass
I'll breathe, and long past midnight, your last kiss.

(Edwin Morgan)

2.19 Answering back

WHAT TO DO

1 The students work in pairs. Each pair works with the same poem (see below).

2 While the students are reading the poem, write up some suggestions such as the following:
   – The writer is a friend of yours and has sent you the poem for comment – how do you reply?
   – You have come across the poem in a magazine. There are certain

questions you would like to ask or comments you would like to make. Note them down and make a rough draft of your letter to the poet.
- You have been asked to translate the poem into your own language. The writer has agreed to help you (in English). Note down the questions you would like to ask him/her, e.g. 'What does he mean when he says we *lead* our lives but don't *own* them?'

3 Each pair selects *one* of the suggestions and works on it for eight to ten minutes. They then join another pair. The one pair is the 'reader', the other the 'writer'. The readers put their questions, the writers must try to answer them. Then roles are reversed.

COMMENTS

1 The element of role-play helps to make the discussion less personal. (The students are not necessarily voicing their own opinions.) It also provides a challenge – to find answers to questions you yourself might have asked!

2 A further exercise in criticism, which we shall describe only in note form, is to present the students with a number of short critical statements on the poem (or poet). For instance:

> The heartiness and fluency of *The Highwayman* earned Noyes
> a popularity beyond that of any of his contemporaries except
> Kipling, but his marked beat and easy rhyme have caused him
> to be relegated today to adolescents.

(See 3.10 for an extract from the poem.) The students are asked to look for examples in the text of, e.g. 'heartiness' or 'easy rhyme', and to discuss the criticism.

□ See also: Criticism (2.18), Translations (2.20), Reactions to texts (1.4), Editor's choice (3.1), Poetry or prose? (2.1).

Bus Stop

Lights are burning
In quiet rooms
Where lives go on
Resembling ours.

The queer lives
That follow us –
These lives we lead
But do not own –

»»→

Stand in the rain
So quietly
When we are gone,
So quietly.

And the last bus
Comes letting dark
Umbrellas out –
Black flowers, black flowers.

And lives go on
And lives go on
Like sudden lights
At street corners

Or like the lights
In quiet rooms
Left on for hours,
Burning, burning.

(Unknown)

2.20 Translations

WHAT TO DO

Find two translations of the same poem, (a) and (b).

1 Read out translation (a) aloud to the whole group. Using the procedure described in Building up from memory (2.7) ask the students to note from memory any fragments of the poem they can recall. Repeat once or twice until they have an almost complete text.
2 Now present the text of translation (b). Working in groups of three, the students work through the passage looking for any strong points of *similarity* and any striking *differences* in the wording. At this stage, they are not directly concerned with the meaning.
3 They are then shown the text of passage (a), and asked to compare the two versions line-by-line, or thought-by-thought. It may help to do this comparison under headings, like this:

	Identical	Similar	Little in common	Quite different
Line/thought 1:		√		

When this is complete, each group compares and discusses its findings with others.

Two translations of Omar Khayyam

a) Here with a Loaf of Bread beneath the Bough
A Flask of Wine, a Book of Verse – and Thou
Beside me singing in the Wilderness
And Wilderness is Paradise enow.

b) A gourd of red wine and a sheaf of poems –
A bare subsistence, half a loaf, not more –
Supplied us two alone in the free desert:
What Sultan could we envy on his throne?

a) The moving Finger writes; and having writ,
Moves on: nor all thy Piety nor Wit
Shall lure it back to cancel half a line
Nor all thy Tears wash out a word of it.

b) What we shall be is written, and we are so.
Heedless of God or Evil, pen, write on!
By the first day all futures were decided;
Which gives our griefs and pains irrelevancy.

4. Here is another example:

a) *Winter*

News I bring:
bells the stag,
winter snow,
summer past;

wind high and cold,
low the sun,
short its course,
seas run strong;

russet bracken,
shape awry,
wild goose raises
wonted cry;

cold lays hold
on wings of bird,
icy time:
this I heard.

(Anon.)

b)   *The Coming of Winter*

> I have news for you; the stag bells, winter snows, summer has gone.
>
> Wind high and cold, the sun low, short its course, the sea running high.
>
> Deep red the bracken, its shape is lost; the wild goose has raised its accustomed cry
>
> Cold has seized the birds' wings; season of ice, this is my news.

(Anon.)

c)   *Season Song*

> Here's a song —
> stags give tongue
> winter snows
> summer goes.
>
> High cold blow
> sun is low
> brief his day
> seas give spray.
>
> Fern clumps redden
> shapes are hidden
> wildgeese raise
> wonted cries.
>
> Cold now girds
> wings of birds
> icy time —
> that's my rime.

(Anon.)

COMMENTS

1   It is advisable not to ask the question 'which version do you like best', as this rarely leads to useful discussion. (Though, on a line-by-line basis it is possible to ask 'which version of this particular thought do you prefer?') The main aim of the exercise is to discuss differences *in the text* rather than to state preferences.

2   One strong advantage of translation is that it allows for the introduction of material from the mother tongue. Students may even be invited to produce their own versions of well-known poems from the mother tongue; these can later be matched against a published translation.

☐ Prose versions of poems (e.g. *The Panther*, see p. 57) would also be suit-able. Also worth trying are short passages from the Bible – King James' version compared with the New English Bible.

3 Working out from the poem

There is a French saying which might be adapted to fit this chapter: 'on cause mieux quand on ne dit pas *causons*'. This means, roughly, 'We talk better when we don't say *let's talk*'. Or in this context: 'We often talk better when we don't say let's talk about the poem'.

In other words, we do not ask the student to *explain* the poem but rather to work with it. In the process, the students will comment on the poem in their own time and in their own way. A poem contains many thoughts, many suggestions, not all of which can be 'grasped' at once. Understanding comes gradually. And often we understand best when we are not making a deliberate effort to understand.

Finally, one brief point: 'understanding' is not all. Students will have little difficulty in understanding, for instance, these lines:

> She lives in a garret
>   Up a haunted stair,
> And even when she's frightened
>   There's nobody to care.

or these:

> I am the man who gives the word,
>   If it should come, to use the Bomb.

But, precisely because they understand the lines, they may have great difficulty in finding 'something to say' about them. That is, if they are asked to *explain* the lines. But if instead they are asked to *react* to them, e.g. through the role-play exercise, they will find that thoughts will be released and they will in fact have 'plenty to say'.

As the title of this chapter suggests, the aim of the activities is to enable the students to *work out* from the poem by relating it to their own experience. And also by extending the theme, as in the Interviews (3.7) or in Themes (3.5, 3.6), along lines of their own choice. Like this, they are taking up from where the poet left off, adding what was not said – but might have been. And, in so doing, coming *back* from time to time to the poem itself.

To summarise: the activities allow the student to work out from the poem in different directions – even to stray quite far! The poem is like a base-camp to which the explorers return, when they choose, with their discoveries.

3.1 Editor's choice

WHAT TO DO

a) Present three or four poems, without revealing the writer's name.

b) The students work in groups of three. The members of each group are to form an editorial board (or panel of judges). Their task will be to select *one* poem from the set for publication (or a prize).

c) The groups decide on their 'identities'. Each group should choose a different identity. This can be done by asking them to choose one of several descriptions, for instance:

 i) You are radio editors looking for a poem suitable for a programme called 'Young Voices', intended for children aged 11–14. The poem will be spoken by a child, not an actor.

 ii) You are editors of a magazine called 'International Economic Survey'. Occasionally you publish a poem which might interest a business-minded reader.

 iii) You are judges at a provincial poetry competition. Your instructions state that 'prizes should be awarded to poems which combine technical skill with originality of thought'. You are selecting the poem for *third* prize.

 iv) You are editors working on a language text-book for foreign learners, to be used by scientists. The author has asked you to help her select a suitable poem for inclusion in the text.

d) The members of each group discuss the poems and make their choice, noting their reasons both for accepting the one poem and for rejecting the others. Even if they are not 'happy' with their choice, it must be made.

e) After deliberation, the groups discuss their decisions with each other.

COMMENTS

a) There are no right or wrong decisions. Each group is judging the poems according to its own needs. It is even possible that one group will accept a poem for the same reason that another rejected it.

b) It is important to stress that a choice *must* be made, even if the poem is 'not quite' suitable (no poem ever will be!). Groups will have time to explain their reservations during the discussion. (And, indeed, they do!)

c) A sample set of poems is given below. However, all poems in the book are suitable for this exercise. Translations would provide another useful source of material.

d) In countries where English is a second language (e.g. India, the Philippines), for identity option (ii) students can be asked to select a magazine or journal which is published in their own country.

□ See also: Using pictures (1.1), Titles (1.4), Illustration (2.9), Translations (2.20), Prose into poem (7.12).

Coat

Sometimes I have wanted
to throw you off
like a heavy coat.

Sometimes I have said
you would not let me
breathe or move.

But now that I am free
to choose light clothes
or none at all

I feel the cold
and all the time I think
how warm it used to be.

(Vicki Feaver)

Transformations

Portion of this yew
Is a man my grandsire knew,
Bosomed here at its foot:
This branch may be his wife.
A ruddy human life
Now turned to a green shoot.

These grasses must be made
Of her who often prayed,
Last century, for repose;
And the fair girl long ago
Whom I often tried to know
May be entering this rose.

So, they are not underground,
But as nerves and veins abound
In the growths of upper air,
And they feel the sun and rain,
And the energy again
That made them what they were!

(Thomas Hardy)

Prisoner and Judge

The prisoner was walking round and round the prison yard.
He had a low forehead and cruel eyes;
You couldn't trust him anywhere.
He dressed up as a judge; he put on a wig and robes
And sat in court in the judge's place.
And everyone said:
    'What a deep forehead he has, what learned eyes!
    How wise he looks!
    You could trust him anywhere.'

The judge was sitting in court in the judge's place.
He had a deep forehead and learned eyes;
You could trust him anywhere.
He dressed up as a prisoner; he put on prisoner's clothes
And walked round and round the prison yard.
And everyone said:
    'What a low forehead he has, what cruel eyes!
    How stupid he looks!
    You couldn't trust him anywhere.'

(Ian Serraillier)

The Universal Good

To do each day our daily task, life's busy course to run,
To do the things that we must do, and leave no thing undone,
To take our place on the stage of life, and play our modest part,
To keep the flame of hope alive, and bright within our heart,
Not to despair when things go wrong, but rather to set them right.
    If this we did, it would do more
    Than politicians ever could
    To bring us peace, an end to war
    And universal good.

(adapted from Patience Strong)

3.2 Everyday things: notes

WHAT TO DO

a) The students work individually. They are given three situations, each
of which requires a note to be written, e.g.
  i) You have to leave home suddenly and have no time to let your
    neighbour know. Write a note explaining very briefly what you

would like him/her to do while you are away (e.g. 'Please feed the cat / collect my mail' etc.).

ii) You are three hours late for an appointment/meeting/rendezvous. Write a note explaining why.

iii) You have been staying in a friend's flat and have consumed a very special cheese which was in the fridge. It is Sunday: you have to leave before he/she returns, and you have no time to replace the cheese. Write a note to leave in the fridge.

b) The time-limit is four minutes. The students should write a note for at least one of the above situations. (If inspired, they may write more.)

c) They now compare notes with at least three other students. While they are doing this, write up the following short poem on the board:

This is just to say

I have eaten
the plums
that were in
the icebox

and which
you were probably
saving
for breakfast

Forgive me
they were delicious
so sweet
and so cold.

(William Carlos Williams)

d) In pairs, the students now try to turn one of the notes into a 'poem' on the lines of the one above. No changes must be made to the original wording of their notes. When ready, they exchange 'note poems' with another pair.

e) Each group of four is invited to read out its best 'note-poem'.

COMMENTS

a) It is important that the students should write out their notes <u>before</u> seeing the poem, otherwise they will merely imitate the model.

b) One should not expect great results. The purpose of the exercise is not to prove that prose can be turned into poetry but to suggest that poetry can be found in everyday things.

□ See also: Newspaper articles (1.4), Jumbled lines (2.5), Prose into poem (7.12).

3.3 Everyday things: news items

a) The students work in pairs or in groups of three. They look at a short poem, preferably one dealing with something that is 'newsworthy'.
b) In their groups, they convert the poem into a news item – a radio or newspaper report. This need not be a faithful account of the poem – they may add or leave out details as they wish.
c) After ten minutes, each group reads its news item aloud.

Here is an example:

i)   *News Item*

        Let us salute the enterprise
        of the man who recently
        made a model pterodactyl,
        very lifelike
        with a little motor
        so that it could fly.

        It cost 700,000 dollars.

        It must have been a tough decision
        considering the other things
        he could have got for 700,000 dollars.

        Think of the guts needed
        not to give it to cancer research
        or starving children.

        But the things of the spirit
        are the things of the spirit.
        You cannot compromise

        Some people were critical
        because the pterodactyl crashed on take-off
        and was smashed to pieces.

        But that is not the point.
        Art is for ever.

        (Michael Swan)

ii)   After months of experiment, an American amateur scientist recently completed a full-scale model of the prehistoric pterodactyl. This bird, with a wing-span of over five metres, is the largest flying creature ever known to have existed.
        The model, powered by battery, was designed to simulate the pterodactyl's flight. Unfortunately, the first – and only – flight ⟫→

ended with the 700,000 dollar model crashing to the ground after a few seconds in the air.

In spite of public criticism, the constructor is determined to repeat his experiment. He has the confidence, all he needs is the money.

☐ Other poems in this book which lend themselves to this are: *A Sad Song About Greenwich Village* (see p. 85), *Landscape with the Fall of Icarus* (see p. 60).

COMMENTS

a) A useful focus for the discussion is: what parts of the poem were left out in the news-reports? And why? What details are given in the reports which are not given in the poem? (e.g. the person's age).
b) The exercise can be done in reverse, by giving the students the news item and asking them to turn it into a poem. Other variants include turning the poem into a telegram / letter / telephone conversation / diary entry, etc.

☐ See also: Newspaper articles (1.4), One at a time (2.10), Contrasts (2.14, 15, 16), and Prose into poem (7.12).

3.4 Everyday things: advertisements

WHAT TO DO

a) Students work in pairs. They read a short poem. This should preferably be one which either describes an object, a place or a person (e.g. Robert Graves' *Face in the Mirror*, Michael Swan's *Pity* (see p. 62)).
b) They then convert the poem into an advertisement. This might be a classified ad. (e.g. Distinguished elderly bachelor with grey hair . . . etc. seeks life companion to share old age etc.) or a full advertisement. Before starting, students must decide what kind of a publication the ad. will appear in and what kind of readership it is aimed at. (Alternatively it might be a radio or TV ad.) They may expand upon the details provided by the poem, or leave them out.
c) After ten minutes, each group either reads out or (in the case of TV ads) performs its ad.

COMMENTS

a) One variation is to divide the class into three main groups. Within each group pairs work on the same poem (i.e. three different poems for the whole class). After the groups have read their ads to each other, they exchange the ads (*not* the poems). Each group then attempts to reconstitute the poem on which the ad. was based.

□ See also: Word portraits (3.9).

3.5 Themes: conversation

WHAT TO DO

a) The students work in pairs. Each pair notes down quickly as many everyday conversational phrases as they can think of, e.g. 'How nice, How kind, How do you do, Lovely weather, I'm *so* sorry, Take care, Lovely seeing you, *Do* keep in touch, I'm afraid we must be going...' etc.

b) Each pair exchanges ideas with at least two other pairs.

c) Present the two poems below. (These are intended merely to help generate ideas.)

d) In groups of three or four, the students devise a short sketch in which the dialogue is made up entirely of ready-made phrases.

COMMENTS

a) Here the poems play a very minor role. They are in a sense merely illustrations for the exercise.

b) The theme of *conversation* in poetry however, is one which is worth exploring further. For this purpose, the exercise above would be useful preparation.

□ Further items might be suggested by other poems in this book, including *Pity* (see p. 62), *There are four chairs around the table* (see p. 28), and *Does he mean me?* (see p. 159). See also: Wole Soyinka, *Telephone Conversation*; Louis MacNeice, *Conversation*, and lines 139–71 of T. S. Eliot's *The Waste Land*.

≫→

Doorstep Duet

Lovely having you!	Lovely seeing you!
Do come again.	We'll give you a ring.

Well, goodbye, goodnight	Well, goodnight, goodbye
Oh, I nearly forgot! . . .	Oh, that reminds me! . . .
Tuesday's all right	We can't make Tuesday
But Friday's out	But Friday we're free
Never mind . . .	Anyway . . .
We'll give you a ring	We'll give you a call

Have you got all you brought?	Have we got all we brought?
Wish you could stay	Must be on our way
Oh, and thanks for the flowers!	Wonderful dinner!
You shouldn't have, really . . .	You really shouldn't have . . .
No trouble at all	The pleasure was ours

Just a minute. I'll switch on the light
    Please don't bother. It's quite all right.
Harold will see you to the car.
    No need, really. It isn't far.
Well, mustn't be keeping you.
    Must let you go.
If there's any change . . .
    . . . we'll let you know.
    Goodnight. Goodbye.
    Do keep in touch.
    Goodbye. Goodnight.
    And thank you *so* much.

Such nice people	I thought they'd never
but oh so slow!	let us go!

(A.D.)

Meaning What?

'I wish . . . '
'You wish what?'
'I wish that I could . . . '
'That you could what?'
'I wish that I could find a
  way to . . . '
'Find a way to what?'
'I wish that I could find a way
  way to tell you . . . '
'To tell me what?'

'I wish that I could find a way
  to tell you that I find you . . . '
'Find me what?'
'Boring! There – I've found it!'
'What . . . ?'

(A.M.)

3.6 Themes: concentration

WHAT TO DO

a) Write up the word CONCENTRATION on the board. Ask the students to note down individually as many moments of intense concentration as they can think of. If necessary, offer a few suggestions to start them off, e.g.:
  – an ice-skater preparing to do a double leap
  – a diver on a high board, about to dive
  – a surgeon about to make the first incision
  – a cat stalking a bird
  – a crane-driver lowering a heavy load into place

b) After five minutes, the students form groups of three and compare their lists. They should now choose *three* of their suggestions and write down, in no more than five sentences, exactly what the person (or animal) does just *before* the moment of concentration, e.g. an athlete – flexes their arms, touches their toes, jogs up and down, settles into place, wipes their forehead, etc.
  Each group now reads out its notes to another group.

c) Write on the board the text of *Flashlight*. Allow time for silent reading and some discussion.

d) Ask the students to concentrate only on the first two lines:

  My flashlight tugs me
  through the dark

  They now look back at their earlier suggestions and try to find for each a phrase which will suggest what is passing through the mind of the person who is concentrating. Finally, each group reads aloud its best suggestions.

COMMENTS

a) The preparation exercises will help the student to think around the theme *before* coming to the poem. And so, to be more alert to what is said.

b) The fourth stage is optional. (It could also be the basis for an out-of-class writing exercise, in which the students would develop the theme of *concentration* in their own way.)

□ See also: Reactions to texts (1.4), Paraphrase (2.17), Illustration (2.9).

Flashlight

My flashlight tugs me
through the dark
like a hound
with a yellow eye,

sniffs
at the edges
of steep places,

paws
at moles'
and rabbits'
holes,
points its nose
where sharp things
lie asleep —

and then bounds
ahead of me
on home ground.

(Judith Thurman)

3.7 Interviews

WHAT TO DO

This exercise is a follow-up to the section on Using recordings (1.3).

a) When preparing for the recording devise a brief series of questions to ask four adults (if possible native-speakers). These all bear on the poem *The Responsibility*. For instance:
  – Do you think Ban-the-Bomb demonstrations have any effect on those *responsible* for atomic tests?
  – Have you ever seen a film showing or simulating the explosion of an atomic bomb? If so, what do you remember most clearly from it?
  – Do you approve or disapprove of atomic tests? Or are you neutral?
  – Can you suggest any ways in which the nuclear threat could be reduced or removed?
b) Before playing the recording, ask the class in groups of three to discuss their own feelings on these questions. Then play the recording and ask them to note the speakers' reactions with the help of this grid. Play the recording several times if necessary.

	Demon- strations?	Film?	Tests?	Suggestions?
Speaker 1				
Speaker 2				
Speaker 3				
Speaker 4				

c) In pairs, the students compare notes. A brief round-up session is held
   to clear up any disagreements. With smaller classes, the students then
   discuss how their own feelings match those of the speakers. With
   larger classes, this is best done in groups of four.
d) Introduce the following prose text and poems, then play the
   recording.

COMMENTS
a) For some, this may be a subject they prefer not to discuss. If at any
   stage some students prefer to be silent, they should not be pressed to
   speak.
b) The advantage of the recording, however, is that it allows the students
   to speak both *objectively* (about what the speakers said) and *sub-
   jectively* (about their own reactions).
□ The poem, *The Responsibility*, could also be effectively used in chapter
   4 (Speaking poetry) e.g. Expression (4.7). The prose extract would
   be extremely suitable for two other exercises – Keywords I (8.10) and

Prose into poem (7.12). See also the poem *At the Bomb Testing Site* in Fractured phrases (2.6).

The Responsibility

I am the man who gives the word,
If it should come, to use the Bomb.

I am the man who spreads the word
From him to them if it should come.

I am the man who gets the word
From him who spreads the word from him.

I am the man who drops the Bomb
If ordered by the one who's heard
From him who merely spreads the word
The first one gives if it should come.

I am the man who loads the Bomb
That he must drop should orders come
From him who gets the word passed on
By one who waits to hear from him.

I am the man who makes the Bomb
That he must load for him to drop
If told by one who gets the word
From one who passes it from him.

I am the man who fills the till,
Who pays the tax, who foots the bill
That guarantees the Bomb he makes
For him to load for him to drop
If orders come from one who gets
The word passed on to him by one
Who waits to hear it from the man
Who gives the word to use the Bomb.
I am the man behind it all;
I am the one responsible.

(Peter Appleton)

The Atomic Tests at Bikini

James Cameron was one of the three British observers invited to witness the first underwater atomic explosions near the Pacific atoll of Bikini in 1946. Here he describes the effects of the second explosion.

For some reason on that second bomb-day my nerves were more ragged, my expectation more intense than when I had leaned against the same ship's rail three weeks before. I had been up since four, listening to the silence. Now I was again on the flydeck, listening to the radio . . .

It was as before. Overhead the planes circling in their courses, drilling and waiting. 'Fifteen minutes before How Hour'. 'One minute before How Hour'. I could see the structures of the target fleet eight miles away, standing up over the horizon line like the silhouette of a castellated city.

'Ten seconds . . . six seconds . . . four seconds, three seconds, two seconds . . . '

It came gently, imperceptibly to begin with; one's heightened senses seemed somehow to decelerate that first subdivided second until one saw, or felt oneself to see, the gradual maturing of an instantaneous thing. There across the field of the lens's view stretched the bowstring horizon of the mid-Pacific, the tautest, straightest line of nature; where this ruled edge met the sky came the flash. Then where the flash had been a ball, a gleaming hemisphere of purest white, a grotesque and momentary bubble, huge and growing huger, a dome rising from the sea. Immediately the forces inside it strained and burst through; there was now no dome but a column, a pillar of water more than half a mile across, a million tons of the Pacific Ocean leaping vertically, silently, soaring upward into the cloud base; one mile, two miles high until it hesitated, dropped lazily back like a mountainous snowman into the terrible cauldron of Bikini lagoon, by now a waste of murk and fog. In that initial moment – though one did not yet know – the battleship *Arkansas* had been tossed into the air like a tin toy, thrown vertically up and over like a caber, like a wafer. She fell back to the bottom, never to be seen again.

If the first bomb had somehow seemed a lesser thing than one had expected, this indeed was infinitely greater. There was a feeling as the enormous water-dome swelled and expanded in perfect symmetry to a monstrous bulk that it would never stop developing, that it would increase indefinitely and overwhelm us, and not only us, but everyone, even the world. Then the outward movement became an upward one, there was the ineffable grace of the column, the weary slowness with which it dripped its million tons back towards the lagoon. And when the waves ribbed over the reef and were absorbed into the smoothness of the sea, the intense realization of the enormity, not of the bomb but of the ocean, this huge expressionless Pacific which could take even an atom bomb, embrace it, and forget it while one looked on.

(James Cameron, *Point of Departure*)

3.8 Dramatisation / role play

WHAT TO DO

a) Try out the exercise Immediate reactions (see p. 25) in Preparing for the poem, chapter 1. As the stimulus word write up either *loneliness* or *neighbours*.

b) After the discussion, ask the students to form groups of four. Each group looks at the text of *A Sad Song About Greenwich Village*. In the group, one person takes the role of the writer (*I*, in the poem), one the part of the old lady (*she*), and the other two the roles of two investigative journalists who have come to find out about how old people live in the city.

c) Each group prepares a short sketch in which the old lady and the younger woman are interviewed *together* by the two journalists. (In the preparation, the two pairs work separately.) Here are some suggestions to help the students get started, but they should be encouraged to add more ideas of their own.

   i) *The two women* should discuss:
       – their names (do they know each other by name?), how old they are, how often they see each other (once a day? once a week?), who their nearest neighbours are;
       – visits (has either ever been inside the other's flat?), everyday problems (noise, climbing the stairs, smells, etc.);
       – why the old lady has not been seen 'since a long time ago';
       – things they have in their flats that are precious to them (does the old lady have a cat?) . . .

   ii) *The two journalists* prepare questions to find out:
       – how long the old lady has been living in the garret; how much money she lives on; what she eats; whether she has a telephone, radio, TV, stove, etc.; how often she has visitors; how good her health is; what she thinks of her neighbours, and how much help she gets from them;
       – whether the younger woman ever visits the old lady; what work the younger woman does; what she thinks of the neighbours and what contact she has with them; how long she has lived in the district, etc.

d) Allow at least ten minutes for preparation. The two pairs then join up, and the journalists ask their questions.

e) The interviews are done once again, with different pairs.

COMMENTS

a) This exercise is an extension of the *theme* of the poem rather than a dramatisation of the text. Considerable freedom can therefore be allowed in building up the details of the old woman's life. For instance, is she really as unhappy as her young neighbour thinks? The poem gives us only one side of the story.

b) It is important to do the interviews *twice*, with different pairs, because the students will become more familiar with their roles and therefore more fluent and better able to *improvise*.

c) A useful variant of this exercise is to suggest different characters who might speak to the old lady. What questions, for instance, would the following ask?
   – a doctor
   – a shop-keeper
   – a young relative (nephew or niece)
   – a tax inspector
   – a historian or research worker
   This idea can also be used in most of the exercises below.

d) In countries where this situation would be unfamiliar or unimaginable, the students can be asked to 'translate' the situation into local terms by previously discussing what would be the local equivalents of, e.g. 'Greenwich Village', 'garret', 'lodging'.

□ See also: Memories (1.2), Newspaper articles (1.4), Using drama and role-play (1.5), Missing lines (2.4), Illustration (2.9), Word-portraits (3.9), Just listen (4.1), That's life (5.2), Everyday things (3.2, 3, 4) and the poem *What has happened to Lulu?* in *Poem into Poem*, chapter 3.

A Sad Song About Greenwich Village

She lives in a garret
   Up a haunted stair,
And even when she's frightened
   There's nobody to care.

She cooks so small a dinner
   She dines on the smell,
And even if she's hungry
   There's nobody to tell.

She sweeps her musty lodging
   As the dawn steals near,
And even when she's crying
   There's nobody to hear.

I haven't seen my neighbour
   Since a long time ago,
And even if she's dead
   There's nobody to know.

(Frances Park)

3.9 Word portraits (role play)

WHAT TO DO

The most suitable poems for this exercise are those which focus strongly on a particular person. The exercise is described in relation to the poem on page 90, but other poems in the book might be used (e.g. *Childhood* (see p. 24).

a) In pairs, the students note down any jobs which they would *not* like to do. Against each job, they note what they find most disagreeable about it. After four or five minutes, each pair exchanges notes with two or three other pairs.

b) Ask all the pairs to note down briefly what they feel are the *advantages* and *disadvantages* of being a museum / art gallery attendant. Allow two to three minutes for discussion.

c) Ask the class as a whole to call out their observations. Note these on the board under separate columns headed Advantages and Disadvantages.

d) Present the Interview sheet (see p. 81). The students check their own comments against those made by the interviewees, and compare them with the comments on the board.

e) Introduce the poem *Still Life* (see p. 90). First the students look for any details in the poem which match either their own comments or the prose passages. Then each pair devises a *short* sketch illustrating an incident with which the woman in the poem might have to deal (e.g. a 'nutter' attacking one of the pictures with a knife, or an old man picnicking on the bench in front of a famous painting). After five minutes, the pairs perform their sketches to each other.

COMMENTS

a) This exercise is an example of what we meant in the introduction to this chapter by saying that the students can 'carry on from where the poem leaves off'. That is, the students are free to use the poem (and the prose texts) as a framework for constructions of their own.

b) It is important to display (on the board or OHP) the students' first comments, *before* they have seen the texts. These comments will later be a valuable point of reference and comparison, and will help to focus discussion of the texts.

c) An alternative approach would be to use the texts as a starting-point for interviews on the theme of *job (dis)satisfaction*. These could be conducted 'live' in the mother tongue with, for example, park attendants, ticket-collectors, waiters and so on in their home town. Each group would then present the results of its research, in English, to the rest of the class.

□ See also: Using pictures (1.1), Using recordings (1.3), Interviews (3.7), Dramatisation/role play (3.8), That's life (5.2), When I'm old (5.5). D. H. Lawrence's poem *After the Opera* would also be suitable here.

Making an exhibition of themselves

A sideways look at the British way of life

There must be hundreds of equally juicy anecdotes told in the privacy of museum staff-rooms where the attendants put their feet up for a few minutes' tea-break. But museum attendants are frustratingly discreet: they take a pride in their good relations with the public, and are ever alert to any breach in that vast amorphous abstract, security.

On duty, they talk to each other like people at a grand cocktail party, constantly glancing over each other's shoulders to see if somebody more important has come in. In the National Gallery, they are provided with chairs, and are required to wear ties; not many hats. In the Natural History Museum, no chairs or ties, all hatted. In the V&A, hats on, ties off (but in the pocket in case the chief warder changes his mind), and very uncomfortable-looking high stools.

The uniform of many attendants also displays a short length of chrome-plated chain, on the end of which is a whistle. This jailer image was empasized as I watched an attendant with a longer bit of chain than usual, patrolling a room full of musical instruments. Every now and then he

⫸→

peered suspiciously into one of the cases, as if to make sure that the sixteenth-century zither imprisoned there was not going to make a desperate bid for freedom.

He was probably just reading the labels. Unless the museum is very small, an attendant cannot relax if there are no visitors. He can't sit down and read a book. The rooms they work in can be very warm in summer, and bitterly cold in winter. "You can't help but learn". I was told. "Often there's nothing to do but walk up and down and look at the exhibits."

This is why most museum attendants are far more knowledgeable than one might expect, and not just from reading labels. In some museums the staff have access to the director's library during night shifts, and are encouraged to dip into its contents.

Where the staff are members of a union, they like new arrivals to join – usually the TGWU, or sometimes the Civil Service Union. They do not talk much about union business. Security again. With some of the nutters around nowadays, you can't be too careful.

There was a time when security was not so tight, and nutters were more benign. A lady came to a National Trust property, armed with a pair of bicycle handlebars. The attendants could not persuade her to part with them, since she said she had been threatened by a man in the garden. She got quieter as she entered a long windowless corridor, until she came to a large painting of a male nude. *"That's him!"* she shrieked, and shot off down the passage.

Being a museum attendant is not a glamorous job but those who do it have a quiet, protective affection both for their museums and the public – even the bossy ones, who yell "Don't touch please!" with all the relish of a pantomime drill sergeant. In Palm Beach, Florida, however, to be an attendant at the newly-opened Henry Flangler Museum carries an enormous social cachet. Their job applications file reads like the Palm Beach social register, and there are 16 Rolls-Royces in the staff car-park.

George Bonilla, a V & A warder, laughed. "It's not like that here," he said. "Even the director comes to work in an old Ford."

Artemis Cooper

Forest ranger

Jack Gould
Attendant for 10 years at
Nottingham Castle.

❛ I shouldn't like to have lived here. Too cold. But there's always somebody visiting the Castle, whatever the weather. It's always an outing if you've got people staying, and in the summer it gets very crowded. People come into the grounds to sunbathe, and into the museum – which is free – to cool off. One of the most popular paintings in our gallery is called *Love's Oracle:* "Ooh it's beautiful; do you have a print of it?" – It costs them 70p for the print, then probably a tenner to get it framed. . .You must always be calm and civil in this job, but the longer you're standing here, the more the silly questions try your patience. If you're standing two feet from the tea room, with your elbow practically in the teapot, someone is bound to come up and ask the way to the cafeteria. And of course Robin Hood's on all the time. "Which part of the castle did Robin Hood live in?, Where can we see his bows and arrows?" But the most common question is the way to the ladies lavatory. You'd be surprised how many different ways there are of saying that. . . . ❜

Touch judge

George Bonilla
Museum Warder for 16 years at the Victoria & Albert Museum.

❛ Most of the public are very pleasant, although they tend to ask for things that aren't here like Magna Carta or the Elgin Marbles. They don't mind their bags being searched – some of them ask for a body-search too. Not all are so well-behaved. I found some young boys smoking in the Music Gallery – in fact I once found a *vicar* smoking there. He said there weren't any No Smoking signs. Then there are the compulsive touchers – they like opening drawers and cupboards. During the Fabergé exhibition, an elderly man with a young lady offered me £10 to let him past the queue. "Haven't you got a price like everyone else?" he said. Lots of people were trying to queue-dodge by saying they knew the Director – the Director never dreamed he had so many friends. Or else they were friends of Bing Crosby, whose binoculars were in the exhibition. There's a 24-hour patrol in the museum, so I'm often on night-shift. There's supposed to be a ghost in the basement – of Warder Clinch, who committed suicide there at the turn of the century. ❜

Eyeballer

Olive Vincent
Museum Invigilator for 12 years. The Ashmolean Museum, Oxford.

❛ I'd rather have the Canaletto in my own home, but Ucello's *Hunt in the Forest* is the most treasured painting here. We had a telephone call about three years ago from someone who threatened to vandalize it, because he didn't approve of blood sports. I once heard a guide describing the artist's technique – she said, 'It's just like darning a sock'. What a thing to say! There was a Russian party in that day – they take their culture very seriously. I remember thinking, I do hope she's not talking to them. People dislike being watched. There was one in particular – soon after I started here: I was keeping an eye on him because I kept hearing rustling paper, as if he were unpacking a picnic. He insisted I call the keeper, and told him he bitterly resented it. The keeper explained that I was just doing my job. There's a man who always comes in when he's in Oxford and never fails to say hello to 'his ladies', as he calls us. And there's a departmental manager from Debenham's, who comes in at Christmas to see the *Flight into Egypt* by Joos de Momper. ❜

House Husband
Anne Beamis
Caretaker/Attendant for 3 years at the King's Lynn Museum of Social History.

❝You can always tell the favourite exhibits by the amount of finger-prints on the glass case. Here, it's the dolls' houses. The kitchen draws a lot of attention, too – children are surprised to hear that water had to be brought to the house in buckets; and some older people remember their mothers using flat-irons, so they are surprised to see flat-irons in a museum! There are two curious objects that are not labelled, sort of accidentally on purpose. That way people's curiosity is aroused, they come and ask about them, and suddenly they have a whole lot more questions they might never have asked. Perhaps because this has been a house, it doesn't feel so much like a museum; people don't feel so shy and reverent. When it gets quite I polish the furniture, or I get a book out of the museum refer-ence library to learn more about the exhibits. And people drop in, sometimes foreign visitors who've been to the museum years before. They poke their heads round the door and say: 'Hello, remember me?' I have a pretty good memory for names, but I can't remember them all. . . .❞

Artemis Cooper

Still Life

On a chair by the door
between Still Life with Flowers
and Portrait of a Lady (artist unknown)
she sits, shading the seconds into minutes,

' . . . and here in the corner (if we could *all*
keep together), Portrait of a Lady –
possibly from Flanders.
Note in particular how, wherever you stand,
you seem to be followed by the eyes,
and how the hint of disillusionment
at the corners of the mouth
is echoed in the folded hands.
Notice too (before we move on)
how well the whole figure
blends with the background . . .'

Eyes weary of galleries
scan the canvas of her face
searching for the frame
and, finding none, move on
noting in passing
how well the whole figure
blends with the background.

On a chair by the door
between Portrait of a Lady (artist unknown)
and Still Life with Flowers
she sits, shading the minutes into hours.

(A.D.)

3.10 Dramatisation (narrative poems)

We have no space, unfortunately, to reproduce in full a long narrative
poem. There are, however, some poems in the book which would be suitable for this exercise: e.g. *The Highwayman* (see below) and *Coat* (see
p. 72). Other suitable poems, which may easily be found in anthologies,
include: Coleridge's *The Rime of the Ancient Mariner*; Browning's *My
Last Duchess*; W. H. Auden's *Victor*, and *The Ballad of Miss Gee*; Oscar
Wilde's *The Ballad of Reading Gaol* . . . and many others.

WHAT TO DO

1 The class is divided into groups of between three and five. Each group
works with *one* stanza (8–10 lines) of the poem.
2 The groups decide among themselves who will act and who will narrate
– or whether they will all act and narrate. In the example below, for
instance, the first stanza could be acted out with only one narrator and
four actors, and the second with four narrators (in chorus) and only
one actress:
(The story: The king's soldiers have come to an inn and seized the land-
lord's daughter, who is in love with 'The Highwayman', who has
promised to return by night . . .)

> *stanza a)*
> They had tied her up to attention, with many a
> sniggering jest;
> They had bound a musket beside her, with the barrel
> beneath her breast!
> 'Now keep good watch!' and they kissed her.
> She heard the dead man say –
> Look for me by moonlight;
> Watch for me by moonlight;
> I'll come to thee by moonlight, though Hell should
> bar the way!

D

3 Working out from the poem

stanza b)

> She twisted her hands behind her; but all the knots
> held good!
> She writhed her hands till her fingers were wet with
> sweat or blood!
> They stretched and strained in the darkness and the
> hours crawled by like years;
> Till now, on the stroke of midnight,
> Cold on the stroke of midnight,
> The tip of her finger touched it! The trigger at
> least was hers!

(Alfred Noyes, from *The Highwayman*)

3 When the groups are ready, they then perform the entire sequence of
the poem, with the stanzas following in order.
4 If possible, the whole class should then listen to a recording of the
poem.

COMMENTS

a) It is difficult, even in the mother tongue, to sustain concentration
when reading or listening to a long poem. This exercise helps to make
the poem more accessible by breaking it down into manageable
portions.
b) The value of *repetition* should be stressed: the students, through
performance, are getting to know the words.

3.11 Visualisation

WHAT TO DO

a) The students work in groups of three. Each group works with one page
of the poem. Their task is to draw up suggestions for a visual
presentation of the poem – this could be either a *film* or a *videotape*.
b) Together they mark the text, looking first for the key images, i.e. the
pictures they feel are most essential. Then they go through it again,
marking down alternative images, i.e. ones which *might* be used, and
any possible sound-effects.
c) Finally, they note any difficulties, for example: what image(s) could be
matched to these lines?

> And every tongue, through utter drought,
> Was withered at the root;
> We could not speak, no more than if
> We had been choked with soot . . .
>
> My lips were wet, my throat was cold,
> My garments all were dank;
> Sure I had drunken in my dreams,
> And still my body drank.
>
> (Coleridge, from *The Rime of the Ancient Mariner*)

d) Each group joins another group. They compare and discuss their
ideas. Any far-fetched ideas should be challenged (e.g. How can you
show a man 'drinking in his dreams'?).

3   Working out from the poem

COMMENTS

a) This will work best if two groups work independently on the same page of text.
b) The students do not need to be asked comprehension questions. By working on the text this way they will come up with their own questions – and answers.

☐ See also: Visualisation (2.8), Just listen (4.1), Taking turns (4.11).

4 Speaking poetry

Because of the many ways in which poetry consciously makes use of sound patterns to achieve its effects (through rhyme, rhythm, metre, etc.), our understanding and enjoyment of most poetry is enhanced when it is read aloud. And, as we pointed out in the introduction, it is one of the few types of writing which it is normal to read aloud – and even to read chorally.

There are then good reasons for exploiting the speaking aloud of poetry in the classroom. In this chapter we suggest some ways in which doing this can be made more interesting and varied.

One word of caution is perhaps called for. There may be initial resistance on the part of some students. It is pointless to try to meet this head on. Those who do not wish to speak will remain silent anyway but there is a good possibility that with persuasion, and through *listening* to others getting enjoyment from it, they will sooner or later join in. In any event, most of the activities here are fun. They are certainly not meant to over-emphasise the serious, portentous nature of poetry recitation, which some of us may remember from our youth!

4.1 Just listen

WHAT TO DO

Read the poem aloud while the class listens, or play a well-recorded version on tape/cassette.

COMMENTS

1 It will usually be advisable to read/play the poem at least three times.
2 It is often helpful if students listen with eyes closed. This usually aids concentration and facilitates the production of mental images.
3 In some cases you may decide that the students should read the text as they listen.
4 Obviously 'just listening' is not usually an isolated activity but is connected in some way with the other things you may wish to do with the poem. (This goes for all the activities in this chapter.) It may, for example, be the first step in the comprehension process.

5 If you are a non-native speaker of English, you may feel reticent about reading poems to your class. There is no reason, however, why you should not do this well, provided you spend a little preparation time in rehearsing the reading. There is, too, an incidental value in doing this: by trying out different readings of a given poem, you will almost always find that new meanings suggest themselves to you.

4.2 Speak-along

WHAT TO DO

Either read or play the poem once to the class. Provide students with the text of the poem (on the board or OHP). Invite them to join in with you / the recording as it is read a second and third time.

COMMENTS

It is important not to force participation. Only those who want to join in should do so. If you tell students to speak softly, more may be encouraged to participate.

4.3 Quick's the word, and sharp's the action

WHAT TO DO

1 Choose a poem in which there are actions or objects which can be mimed or otherwise conveyed through hand or face movements. Here is one possible example:

Child's Nightmare

One is a small child who hides on the floor.
Two is the bogey who knocks on the door.
Three are the windows that creak in the night.
Four are the pillows that hide me from sight.
Five are the fingers that grip on my arm.
Six are the prayers I say against harm.
Seven are the footsteps that thud in the hall.
Eight are the heartbeats I hear as I fall.
Nine are the hot tears that gush from my eye.
Ten is my number. I know I must die.   (A.M.)

2 Read it through line by line. For each line students agree on a mimed action. In some cases, these may be directly related to the action (e.g. knocking on the door). In others, they may be more symbolic (e.g. palms together for prayer).

3 Read it again, relatively slowly. Students match the appropriate gesture to each line as it is read.

COMMENTS

1 Younger students are generally very willing to engage in this activity. But even apparently inhibited groups quickly warm to it. No one is threatened by it, and all can participate without, in this case, having to speak.
2 One possible variation is to divide the class into groups of five. Each group then decides upon its own set of gestures. You then read the poem for each group in turn, as group members perform the actions they have chosen.
3 A further variation, especially in larger classes, is to divide the class into groups of ten. Within each group, students take one line each and decide on a suitable gesture/mime. Each group then performs the poem as it is read.
4 If they feel confident enough, one student in each group can read the poem, while the others perform the actions.

4.4 Pronunciation poems

WHAT TO DO

1 Keep a note over the weeks of words which your students have difficulty in pronouncing. Each student can also be asked to make a list of his/her own difficulties. When you have collected about 30 words, try this exercise.
2 Ask each student to call out *two* words with which he/she has consistent trouble. Write these up on the board or OHP. At the end, add any words from your own list which have not been mentioned.
3 In groups of three or four, the students select any of the words they wish and combine them into a short poem, to which they must give a *title*. For instance:

History	*Bed-rules*
Gold thrones	Soft bed
Cold stones	sleep light
Old bones	Hard bed
	sleep tight!

》》→

Shellbound	Quarrel	
The tortoise	His	
in his tortoise-shell	word	her
has his haven	hard	heart
and his hell		hurt

4 The groups exchange their ideas.
5 A selection of the short poems is written up for recitation in chorus.

COMMENTS

1 We are not suggesting that pronunciation can be 'taught' through poetry (can pronunciation be taught at all?). But there is no doubt that poetry can help to make what is often called 'pronunciation drill' more enjoyable and less like an army exercise.
2 The idea for this activity was first developed in China, with a group of near-beginners, all of whom were scientists. The words in the poems reflect their difficulties (e.g. with long vowel sounds, such as the *o* in *bones*, and consonant endings such as the *t* and *d* in *heart* and *head*). Clearly, with other nationalities different difficulties would emerge.

□ See also: Drip, drop, drizzle (6.2), Traditional rhymes (5.9), and Haikus (5.10).

4.5 All together

WHAT TO DO

1 Choose a poem with a refrain. Rehearse the whole class in reading the refrain aloud together.
2 When they are confident, and used to keeping pace with each other, read the stanzas yourself and ask the students to come in with the refrain. Here is a possible example:

The Prince

The Prince is due in town today:
Whole streets have been cordoned off.
The folk are out in force:
There are many schoolchildren.
How well we know him, our old friend the Prince!
We have photographs stored:
He has been allotted pages
In every family album.
    Three cheers for the Prince!
    Hip-hip . . . Hip-hip . . . Hip-hip . . .

Our Prince is a good man,
He has led a good life; and now,
At long last, he is bringing the Princess
Of his choosing – a beautiful girl –
To be amongst us, to be amongst
His favourite countrymen.
The bells of the town
Cannot peal her beauty.
> Three cheers for the Princess!
> Hip-hip . . . Hip-hip . . . Hip-hip . . .

He has made speeches, our King-to-be,
Attacking the managers:
He is on the side of working people:
Many hardened republicans
Have been converted.
How he must trust us, our King-to-be,
To be bringing the Princess
And the Young Prince, his son!
> Three cheers for the Young Prince!
> Hip-hip . . . Hip-hip . . . Hip-hip . . .

The convoy is turning into the High Street:
It is black, and thrilling the waving crowd.
His bodyguards, like circus dogs,
Jostle for toeholds on the bumpers
Of the royal limousine.
Above the procession, through the
Upper windows of the Guildhall,
Trained observers signal to the bodyguards.
> Three cheers for the bodyguards!
> Hip-hip . . . Hip-hip . . . Hip-hip . . .

Wait! There is a scuffle by the clocktower!
Police are running – ten, twenty:
They are taking hold of youngsters,
They are dragging them to parked vans.
A woman is protesting:
The vans are taking off at speed!
Surely, there has been a terrible mistake –
They seem far too young to be managers.
> Three cheers for our youngsters!
> Hip-hip . . . Hip-hip . . . Hip-hip . . .

(J. R. Hobbs)

COMMENTS

1 Rehearsing the refrain is important, to avoid a ragged performance. It is at this time that students can decide whether some refrains or lines should be spoken more loudly or softly to heighten the overall effect.
2 When students are more used to this activity you might divide them into two groups: one to read the refrains and one to read the stanzas.

☐ See also: That old refrain (8.2).

4.6 From memory

WHAT TO DO

1 Choose a poem which is not too long. For example:

> ### Advice to the Heart
>
> Avoid pain; remain
> hidden, within
> protecting bone
> and muscle.
>
> Do not attempt
> to celebrate the blood
> but be content
> just to circulate it
> corpuscle by corpuscle.
>
> A heart that beats
> to burst the brain's
> frail bubble,
> dances in the streets
> trailing arteries and veins
> in reckless procession
>
> is asking for trouble
>
> (Vasantha Surya)

2 Individually students write out the poem and divide it up into sense-groups by marking them lightly with a pencil.

> e.g. Avoid pain;/remain
> hidden,/within
> protecting bone
> and muscle./

3 They then practise, to themselves, speaking the poem by gradually

building up the sense groups, like this:

- Avoid pain;
- Avoid pain;/remain
  hidden,/
- Avoid pain;/remain
  hidden,/within
  protecting bone
  and muscle./
  etc.

They should practise this cumulative type of reading until the poem has been memorised.

4 They then work in groups of three. Each student gives his own reading to the other two. This can either be done by reading the poem from start to finish, or by gradual accumulation (as in 3 above).

COMMENTS

1 The activity can be made more varied if several different poems are used, so that, in the group reading, each student is reading a different poem.
2 This type of cumulative reading has proved very useful as a way of absorbing, in a very literal sense, a new poem. By focusing on sense groups rather than 'lines', it draws attention to meaning.
3 This could well be set as a homework assignment.

□ Other poems in this book which could be used in this activity include: *This is just to say* (see p. 74), *Meaning What?* (see p. 78).

4.7 Expression

WHAT TO DO

1 Choose a poem which you think lends itself to reading with changes of pace and loudness (W. H. Auden's *Night Mail*, S. T. Coleridge's *The Rime of the Ancient Mariner*, Belloc's *Tarantella* are good examples).
2 Provide students with the text of the poem and decide with them, through discussion, which lines should be speeded up, which slowed down, which spoken louder and which softer.
3 When this is agreed, mark the text to remind the students when to speak louder etc. They then read the poem aloud chorally in the way agreed upon. Here is an example which works well:

≫→

Mornings

Rustling sheet,	(*Start with whisper*)
Shuffling feet,	
Creaking bones,	
Stifled groans,	(*gradually*
Chirping, crowing	*speaking*
Noses blowing,	*louder*)
Toilets flushing,	
Bath taps gushing,	
Coffee cups clatter,	
Breakfast chatter,	
Neighbours singing,	
Telephones ringing,	
Radios tuning,	
Traffic booming,	
Motorbikes thrumming,	
Power drills drumming	
Jet planes thunder –	
I just wonder	(*very soft again*)
At the NOISE!	(*shout*)

(A.M.)

COMMENTS
1 For the performance, it helps if you indicate the lines as they are read. This helps to keep the students speaking together.
2 An alternative procedure is to divide the class into groups of five. Each group then decides for itself how to vary pace etc. Groups then perform their poem.

4.8 Moods

WHAT TO DO
1 Choose a relatively short poem. For example:

Widowhood

She's over it by now, they say.
How can they tell?
She's over it by now,
And doing well.

Though I am still frozen,
And thawing is hell,
She's over it by now, they say,
And doing well.

(Catherine Woods)

2 Divide the class into five groups. Each group is allotted an adjective describing a mood – angry, cynical, anxious, suspicious, excited etc. Groups then decide on how to interpret the poem to convey the feeling of the adjective they have been given.
3 Each group nominates one reader, who speaks the poem to the whole class.

COMMENTS

1 This is clearly a fairly advanced activity and can only be done with classes which have already surmounted the more basic problems of pronunciation and phrasing.
2 By requiring students to think themselves into an attitude it reveals the importance of differing interpretations of the same words.

□ Other poems in this book which might be used include *There are four chairs around the table* (see p. 28), *When I am old* (see p. 55).

4.9 In character

WHAT TO DO

1 Find a poem which is in the form of a dialogue. There are many to choose from. Here are two examples:

Goodbye

'Don't lie', she said.
'I try', he said.
'My eye', she said.
'Don't cry', he said.
'I'll die', she said.
'Oh my!' he said.
'Goodbye!' she said.

(A.M.)

≫→

All there is to know about Adolph Eichmann

EYES	:	Medium
HAIR	:	Medium
WEIGHT	:	Medium
HEIGHT	:	Medium
DISTINGUISHING FEATURES	:	None
NUMBER OF FINGERS	:	Ten
NUMBER OF TOES	:	Ten
INTELLIGENCE	:	Medium

What did you expect?
Talons?
Oversize incisors?
Green saliva?
Madness?

(Leonard Cohen)

2 If the class is mixed, allot all the woman's lines in *Goodbye* above to the females in the class and all the man's lines to the males. You the teacher speak the 'She said' 'He said' parts.
3 In discussion, decide *how* the lines are to be spoken. For example, 'Don't lie' might be in anger, in disappointment, naggingly etc., 'Goodbye!' with steely resolution, or in tears etc.
4 Perform the poem.

COMMENTS

1 The discussion phase, whether conducted with the whole class, or in groups, is extremely important. In deciding on how to speak the lines, the students are in effect coming towards an interpretation of the poem. This personal interpretation of the writer's intentions involves a much deeper process of understanding than mere comprehension of the surface meaning. The very fact of obliging students to decide on how lines are to be spoken involves them directly in decisions of interpretation.
2 Dialogue poems like these may of course be done in pairs, or with small groups taking a part each, or with the class divided into two halves, as suggested above.

□ One very good source of poems to perform in this way are the poems in To your face / Behind your back (8.8). Some poems offer especially rich possibilities since they include up to five characters e.g. Adrian Mitchell's *Giving Potatoes*; *The Responsibility* (see p. 82).

4.10 Sound effects

1 Choose a poem which includes a largish number of words which describe sounds. A good example is *Mornings* (see p. 102). Here is another possibility:

In the Kitchen

In the kitchen
After the aimless
Chatter of the plates,
The murmurings of the gas,
The chuckle of the water pipes
And the sharp exchanges
Of knives, forks and spoons,
Comes the serious quiet,
When the sink slowly clears its throat
And you can hear the occasional rumble
Of the refrigerator's tummy
As it digests the cold.

(John Cotton)

2 In groups of six, students decide which words might be accompanied by a sound (e.g. clatter, groans etc.). They experiment with a 'group sound' for each of these.
3 Two students from each group rehearse reading the poem together. The other four insert the sounds at the appropriate places. Groups then perform the poems for each other.

COMMENTS

1 Obviously the procedure may be varied. For example:
   – the teacher reads while the class produces the sound effects;
   – one group reads, while another makes the effects;
   – in pairs, one student reads while the other makes the sounds.
2 This activity offers some scope for the unrulier elements to produce chaos. One way of checking this is to set short time-limits on the rehearsal periods. Another is to ask students to rehearse their sounds at home before performance!

□ See also: Visualisation (2.8).

4.11 Taking turns

WHAT TO DO

1 Choose a poem in which the lines can be spoken separately without distorting the sense. Here is an example:

The Pessimist

Nothing to do but work,
    Nothing to eat but food,
Nothing to wear but clothes
    To keep one from going nude.

Nothing to breathe but air,
    Quick as a flash 'tis gone;
Nowhere to fall but off,
    Nowhere to stand but on.

Nothing to comb but hair,
    Nowhere to sleep but in bed,
Nothing to weep but tears,
    Nothing to bury but dead.

Nothing to sing but songs,
    Ah, well, alas! alack!
Nowhere to go but out
    Nowhere to come but back.

Nothing to see but sights
    Nothing to quench but thirst,
Nothing to have but what we've got,
    Thus thro' life we are cursed.

Nothing to strike but a gait,
    Everything moves that goes.
Nothing at all but common sense
    Can ever withstand these woes.

(Ben King)

2 Number the lines in the poem and allot one per student. (If this does not quite work out, some students may work in pairs.)
3 Student 1 now reads line 1, Student 2, line 2 etc. through the poem.

COMMENTS

1 There are of course alternative ways of doing this. For example, students can work in groups of eight. They decide who is to read each line

(some will read more than one) and then perform the poem as a group. Alternatively, the class may be divided into two large groups, which speak alternate lines of the poem.

2 A further alternative is to divide the class into six groups for 'The Pessimist'. If there are exactly 24 students in the class it is perfect – one line per student. If there are more, give some lines to two students.) The first read-through is quite slow, the second faster, the third faster still, etc. This accelerated reading can help many students to 'get their tongues' round the words.

□ See also : *The Responsibility* (p. 82), *Mornings* (p. 102).

4.12   Round and round

WHAT TO DO

1 Choose a poem of not more than six lines. The lines should be of equal metric length (e.g. Goodbye – see p. 103).
2 Divide the class into four groups. Group 1 begins to read the poem. As soon as they reach the end of line 1, Group 2 starts on it. As soon as Group 2 reaches the end of line 1, Group 3 starts in on it, and so on. When Group 1 reaches the end of the poem, they go back to the beginning again without a break. Each group will read through the poem three times.

COMMENTS

1 It may help to explain that this is a round, if students are familiar with rounds in their own cultures.
2 Longer poems can be tried once students have got the idea. Possible ones to try from this book include: *Song of the Unhappy Wife* (see p. 140), *As Illogical as Love* (see p. 138), *Mornings* (see p. 102), *Child's Nightmare* (see p. 96).
3 A slight variation is to have Group 1 read a whole verse before Group 2 comes in. This would work with short verses (e.g. *Coat* (see p. 72) or *Island* (see p. 109).

4.13 Echoes

WHAT TO DO

1 Choose a shortish poem, or part of a poem. Here is an example which works well:

⟫→

A Black Jubilee

A broken smile.
A rotten face.
A naughty heart.
A torn affair.
Deathlike noise.
Funeral bells!

(A.M.)

2 Divide the class into two equal halves, A and B. Explain that Group A is to read the lines, pausing briefly at the end of each. Group B is to act as the 'echo'. They will simply repeat, more softly, the final word or phrase of each line.
3 Groups then exchange roles, Group A becoming the 'echo'.

COMMENTS

This 'echo' effect can enhance the performance of a poem. Clearly the teacher must exercise some care in the choice of poem, as it does not work equally well with all poems. In this book, it could be tried with *If I might be an ox* (see p. 49). Here is another example:

To M.M.

The first time
we met as strangers
We parted as friends

The second time
we met as friends
We parted as lovers

The last time
we met as lovers
We parted as friends

We did not meet
again
We are now
not even friends

(Gerald England)

4.14 'Sing we and chant it'

WHAT TO DO

1 Choose a poem which lends itself to group speaking as a chant. Here is an example:

Island

On the island they ran
They ran on the sand
They ran on the shore
At the edge of the sea

They ran in a pattern
A pattern of eight
Two circles that touch
And are touched by the sea

Round the island they ran
They ran round twin hills
Twin hills that rise
That rise from the sea

Round the island they ran
They ran on and on
Son followed father
Father led son

They ran in the sand
The sand by the sea
Son leading father
Father after son

On the island they run
They run on the sand
They run on the shore
At the edge of the sea.

(Tim Dowley)

2 Students work in groups of four. Each group decides how they will read it so as to give it the maximum rhythmical effect.
3 Groups perform the chant to each other.

COMMENTS

1 Many variations can be worked on this activity. Students may chant alternate lines. Or vary pace, loudness or intensity.
2 They may also permutate the order of lines in the poem to obtain an

almost hypnotic repetitive effect. For example:

> On the island they ran
> At the edge of the sea.
> They ran in a pattern
> They ran round twin hills
> They ran on the shore
> Two circles that touch . . .

☐ One excellent source of material and ideas is Carolyn Graham's *Jazz Chants* (see Bibliography). See also Thomas Nashe's *I am sick, I must die* . . .

A NOTE ON RECITATION

Students should be encouraged from the start to recite poems aloud to others in their group or class. These may be published poems, or poems produced by the student or their group.

In order to help students do this better, you might encourage them to ask themselves these questions before they embark upon the reading:
a) Does the poem rhyme? Is it a regular or an irregular rhyme-scheme?
b) Is there a regular rhythmic beat or metre to the poem?
c) Do all the lines stop at the end, or do some of them flow over into the next line?
d) Which words or syllables do I need to stress most heavily?
e) Where should I put the pauses to get the best effect? And how long should they be?
f) Which parts should I speak louder, which softer? And which faster, which slower?
g) If there is a rhyme-scheme, how heavily should I emphasise it?
h) If there is a regular metre, how obvious should I make it in my reading?
i) What is the mood of the poem? Does my reading communicate this mood?
j) Does my reading of the poem distort its meaning in any way?

One of the problems in reading poetry aloud in English is that people come to it with pre-conceived notions about the conventions to be employed. A declamatory, Bardic style of reading is all too often the result. In fact, a great deal of poetry, especially contemporary poetry, is relatively unhistrionic, and much more conversational in tone.

Because such devices as rhyme, metre and so on are employed, the temptation to the reader is to lay stress on them at the expense of the sense. The result is a 'tum-ti tum-ti tum' effect. In fact English poetry relies for much of its effect on a tension between its syntax and its metrical regularity. The syntactical pattern, which is conveying the meaning, will not always fit precisely into the metrical pattern, which is conveying the form. The skilful reader manages to keep these two forces in balance, and pays just enough attention to metre and rhyme for us to notice they are there, but never at the expense of the meaning.

The best advice to a learner driver is 'Keep your eyes on the road'. This is not to say the driver does not need to change gear, accelerate, move the steering wheel etc. Likewise, the best advice we can offer in reading a poem is 'Keep your mind on the meaning'. This is again not to say the reader does not need to pay attention to rhyme, rhythm, assonance and so on. The questions above should help readers to get their priorities straight.

5 Writing – using models

The next four chapters are devoted to techniques for developing the writing of poems by the students themselves. We firmly believe, on the basis of experience with very varied groups of learners, that this is not only feasible, but also valuable in extending their range of language skills.

Developing this kind of writing, as opposed to purely expository writing, offers at least four advantages:–

– it offers many opportunities for genuine interaction between students, as they formulate ideas, discuss and improve drafts, and edit each other's materials.
– it requires learners to adopt a 'hands on' approach, in which they manipulate and explore the limits of the language they possess. This helps to break down the excessive awe in which the foreign language, and especially its literature, is all too often held.
– it builds learner confidence. Once the students have realised that they can produce successful poems, there is a qualitative leap in their motivation.
– by changing students from observers, looking in, into participants, looking out, it helps give them a feel for what is involved in the construction of poems. This direct experience of writing gives access to a kind of understanding of the writing process which no amount of indirect description can offer.

The techniques in this chapter offer the students a good deal of support through providing models to emulate or stems to guide. In this way they can feel relatively secure about the form of what they are writing and can concentrate on ideas.

5.1 Stems

WHAT TO DO

1 Students work individually to begin with. Each one writes a series of sentences, which are true for him/her, following this pattern:
   I have forgotten what...
   I   "   "   who...
   I   "   "   why...
   I   "   "   how to...

112

| I | " | " | where ... |

I   "   "   where ...
I   "   "   when ...
I   "   "   whether ...
etc.

2 In pairs, students compare notes and choose their best items for combination into a poem. They should give the poem a title. Here is an example:

Alienation

I have forgotten what I came to do.
I have forgotten who my friends are.
I have forgotten why I bother to get up.
I have forgotten how to write the simplest word.
I have forgotten where my home is.
I have forgotten when to speak.
I have forgotten whether I exist.

3 Pairs then join each other to form groups of four and discuss each other's versions.

COMMENTS
1 The 'stem' can obviously be varied in many ways. For example:
Who knows what ... ? (where, why etc.)
This is the place where I ...
This is the time when I ...
This is the way I ...
You are the reason why I ...
I wonder who ... (where, what, etc.)
etc.
2 An alternative is to ask students to work on one idea only, e.g. I have forgotten who ... Each one writes five sentences on this pattern before comparing with a neighbour.

□ This exercise is very similar to That's life (5.2).

5.2 'That's life'

WHAT TO DO

1 Write up a number of abstract nouns on the board, e.g. *loneliness, boredom, hope*. Ask for further suggestions from the students.
2 Individually, the students write down any personal associations they have with the words. These should be *concrete* rather than abstract

associations, and written as continuations of the stem:
Boredom *is* . . . ,
Loneliness *is* . . .,
e.g. Boredom is listening to the same story for the third time.
Loneliness is Sundays dragging in the park.
3   In pairs, they now select one theme-word, and combine their associations into a poem, such as:

Loneliness is . . .

Loneliness is a telephone that never rings.
Loneliness is a songbird that never sings.
Loneliness is cold sheets on a cold bed.
Loneliness is being hungry though well-fed.
Loneliness is Sundays moping in the park.
Loneliness is sobbing in the dark.

Frustration is . . .

Queueing for the toilet on an aeroplane.
Hunting for keys at the bottom of your bag.
Losing your last coin in the public call-box.
Being caught in a traffic-jam when you're late for a meeting – and
Discovering, as you slam the front door, that you've left your keys
        inside!

COMMENTS

Pictures can also be effectively used as a stimulus in this exercise.

5.3 'I don't like . . .'

WHAT TO DO

1   In pairs, the students add as many endings as they can to the stem 'I don't like', using verbs ending in *-ing*,
e.g.
I don't like swimming in cold water.
I don't like peeling potatoes.
2   In groups of four, they compare lists and arrange ten of their dislikes in the order that satisfies them best.
3   Each group of four reads out its piece as a chorus, either speaking each line together, or alternating with one line spoken by a solo voice, the next in chorus.

COMMENTS

1 This exercise is particularly suitable for beginners and intermediate students as it gives useful practice in the use of -ing forms.
2 In the choral recitation, some lines could be spoken with '*I* don't like . . .' Others with '*We* don't like . . . ' This will help to give variety to the chant.
3 Some alternative stems are: 'I wish I didn't have to . . . ', 'I hate . . . ', 'If only . . . '. These offer a wider variety of endings.

5.4 'I wish I . . . '

WHAT TO DO

1 Begin by asking the students individually to think of ways of completing a sentence beginning 'I wish I . . . '. They should think, for instance, of things they wished they could do, be, have, become etc. And also of things they wished they did *not* do or did not have to do (e.g. 'I wish I didn't have to get up at 6 a.m.'). It is important to make each sentence as personal and as specific as possible.
2 When they have thought of about ten different sentences, they compare notes with two or three others.
3 Then, in groups of three, they select any *eight* sentences and shape them into a piece of free verse. They may, of course, adapt their original wording. An example of what might be produced is:

> I wish I had a telephone
> I wish I knew how to ride a horse
> I wish I could fill out my income-tax form on my own
> I wish I didn't have to clean the house
> I wish I could understand Plato and Marx
> I wish I didn't hate public parks

(Workshop)

COMMENTS

1 The model given above can be adapted and made more flexible by suggesting other openings, such as: 'If only . . . ', 'Wouldn't it be wonderful if . . . ', 'Why can't . . . ', 'One day, I'll . . . ' etc.

⟫→

115

Reflections at Dawn

I wish I owned a Dior dress
Made to my order out of satin.
I wish I weighed a little less
And could read Latin,
Had perfect pitch or matching pearls,
A better head for street directions,
And seven daughters, all with curls
And fair complexions.
I wish I'd tan instead of burn
But most, on all the stars that glisten,
I wish at parties I could learn
To sit and listen.

I wish I didn't talk so much at parties.
It isn't that I *want* to hear
My voice assaulting every ear,
Uprising loud and firm and clear
Above the cocktail clatter.
It's simply, once a doorbell's rung
(I've been like this since I was young)
Some madness overtakes my tongue
And I begin to chatter . . .

I wish I didn't talk so much
I wish I didn't talk so much
I wish I didn't talk so much,
When I am at a party.

(Phyllis McGinley)

2 Both the above examples rhyme. The students' versions do not have to rhyme, though it adds to their impact if they do.

5.5 'When I am old . . .'

WHAT TO DO

1 Students work individually. Ask them to imagine what it will be like when they are old, and what they will do then. We all know that for many people, old age is a time when they feel free of conventional restrictions, so they feel able to behave in more adventurous ways than when they were younger.
2 They then write down a series of sentences beginning:
'When I am old I shall . . . '

3 Working in groups of three they then share their ideas, pick out the best
   ones and arrange them as a poem. Here is an example:

When I'm Old

I'll read a lot less and learn a lot more.
I'll picket against H-Bombs and sleep on the floor.
In crowds of the dead I'll learn to be alone.
I'll let it ring – never answer the phone.
I'll remember faces, never misplace my glasses,
Make clumsy love to experienced lasses.
With maudlin scorn I'll remember my wife,
Read Ogden Nash and talk about Life,
Have a hearty laugh and smell ashes on my breath
I'll walk upright and slip into death.

(Student)

COMMENTS

1 This particular variant can be used as a way into Stevie Smith's *When
   I am an old woman I shall wear purple* . . .
2 Alternative starting points for the exercise of private fantasy or public
   imagination might be:
   – When the exams are over I'm going to . . .
   – When I get married I'll . . .
   – When I have children I won't . . .
   – If the poor were all rich . . .
   – If the rich were all poor . . .
   – The day the sun went out . . .
   – If I were invisible I'd . . .
   – The day the politicians told the truth . . .
   etc.

5.6 'What I love about . . . '

WHAT TO DO

1 Ask the students individually to draw up a list of things they LOVE and
   things they HATE. They then compare the lists with at least one other
   person, and discuss the reasons for their feelings.
2 Write up the following on the blackboard:
   – What I hate about rain is its . . .
   – What I hate about philosophy is its . . .
   – What I love about precious stones is their . . .
   – What I hate about diamonds is their . . .

 – What I love about egg and bacon is its . . .
 – What I love about a cloud is its . . .
Ask students individually to complete these lines in their own way.
Then compare answers with the whole group.
3 Now, write up this fragment of a poem on the board:

> What I hate about rain is its sneer.
> What I hate about philosophy is its pursed lip.
> What I love about semi-precious stones is their preciousness.
> What I hate about diamonds is their mink.
> What I love about bacon-and-eggs is its predictability.
> What I love about a cloud is its unpredictability.

(*A View of Things*, Edwin Morgan)

Discuss briefly with the whole group how different it is from their own
versions. What makes it so unusual? Can they make any sense of the
comparisons? What connection is there between, for instance, *rain* and
sneer? What is *predictable* about bacon and eggs? etc.
4 Working in pairs, the students take any *ten* of the words on their lists
and work them into a short poem. Each line should begin:
'What I love (or hate) about X is . . . '
When they have finished, they read their poems aloud.

COMMENTS

Even students with only a modest command of English can enjoy doing
this exercise. It is important that the results be compared or read aloud,
as many students will have chosen the same nouns for the first half of the
line (e.g. flowers, spring, my brother/sister), but usually with different
associations.

☐ Here is another poem which could be treated in a similar way:

Without You

> Without you every morning would be like going back to work
>   after a holiday
> Without you I couldn't stand the smell of the East Lancs Road . . .
> Without you Public Houses would be public again
> Without you the Sunday Times colour supplement would come
>   out in black-and-white
> Without you they'd forget to put the salt in every packet of crisps
> Without you all the streets would be one way the other way . . .

(Adrian Henri)

5.7 'I like that stuff...'

1 Ask the students to call out the names of any *substances* (e.g. wood, wool, plastic, paper, butter). Write their suggestions up on the board. About twenty will be needed.

2 Working in pairs, the students now draw up a short list of *objects* associated with each substance, for example:
paper: books, boats (as in paper boat) tickets;
glass: windows, spectacles, eyes
etc.

3 They then choose two or three of the examples and work them into short rhythmic pieces, following the same pattern, like this:

Silk	*Oil*
Parachutists depend on it	Chips are fried in it
Lovely ladies spend on it	Feet slide on it
Silk	Oil
I love that stuff	I love that stuff

or *Paper*

Poets scribble
  on it
Babies dribble
  on it
Paper
I like that stuff

or *Glass*	*Water*
Windows are filled with it	Holy men walk on it
Drinks are spilled from it	Lecturers talk on it
Glass	Water
I love that stuff	I like that stuff

If possible, the first two lines should rhyme or at least have the same rhythm. (The idea is drawn from *I like that stuff* by Adrian Mitchell.)

⟫→

I like that stuff

Lovers lie around it
Broken glass is found in it
Grass
I like that stuff

Elephants get sprayed with it
Scotch is made with it
Water
I like that stuff

Clergy are dumbfounded by it
Bones are surrounded by it
Flesh
I like that stuff

(Adrian Mitchell)

COMMENTS

1 This is a useful exercise for practising the passive in a meaningful way. There is, however, no need to restrict the students to this one form. It is important to allow plenty of time for discussion, as it is then that the students will have the chance to try out various ways of expressing their ideas.
2 An entertaining way of rounding off the exercise is to ask each pair to read out the first *two* lines of any of their pieces, and for the group as a whole to supply the last two lines – in chorus!
3 A variant is to introduce other verbs in the last line, e.g. I hate / I'm afraid of / I can't stand / I need that stuff.

5.8 Pom pom pom pom

WHAT TO DO

1 Choose a short piece of music with a very highly marked rhythmic pattern. (Perhaps the best example to start with is the opening bars of Beethoven's Symphony No. 5.) Working with the whole class, elicit suggestions for words to accompany the first four notes. for example:

Pom	Pom	Pom	Pom
I	want	it	now.
or You	did	it	wrong.
(etc.)			

2 When students have got the idea of writing words to fit the music, ask them to work in pairs to write words for the whole musical extract. For example, the opening passage to the Beethoven can be conceived as a dialogue:

A I say it's wrong.
  I say it's wrong.
B Oh no it's not.
  Oh no it's not.
  Oh no it's not.
A Oh yes it is.
  Oh yes it is.
  Oh yes it is.
B I say it's no . . . t.
A I say it i . . . s.
B I say it's not!
A It is!

3 Students then perform their words for each other in time to the music. Suggested improvements are usually forthcoming at this stage!

COMMENTS

1 The use of music draws attention more emphatically to the importance of the rhythmic beat. Putting words to this beat, like some other exercises in this book, constrains students to search their language repertoire till they find something which fits. This is valuable in helping to develop a feel for what the language will bear rhythmically.

2 Other sources of music for this exercise include:
   – operatic arias (The Magic Flute is a good source). The original words are of course usually in Italian, German or French. Students simply replace them with English words which fit the rhythm. They do not need to translate.
   – Schubert Lieder. The same comments apply.
   – pop songs. Again the original words can be replaced.
   – hymn tunes. Stevie Smith wrote a number of her poems to hymn tunes, including *Faces*, the first verse of which goes:–

   There is a face I know too well,
   A face I dread to see,
   So vain it is, so eloquent
   Of all futility.

   This was to be sung to the tune of 'There is a Green Hill Far Away'. (Rudyard Kipling also composed many of his poems to the tunes of songs, often music hall ditties!)

3 A variant of this exercise is to ask students to think of three pairs of rhyming words e.g. old–cold, track–back, lean–mean. They then write a short poem or song using these as the end words for each line. The song is then adapted to the rhythm of a traditional folk melody of their own culture, and performed.

121

5.9 Traditional rhymes

1 Introduce a traditional rhyme, song, ballad or refrain. This will be used as a model for adaptation. Many suitable rhymes can be found in I. and P. Opie's *The Lore and Language of School Children*. For example:

 a)   One, two, buckle my shoe
       Three, four, shut the door
       Five, six, pick up sticks
       Seven, eight, lock the gate
       Nine, ten, start again.

 b)   Monday's child is full of grace
       Tuesday's child is fair of face.
       Wednesday's child is loving and giving
       Thursday's child works hard for a living.,
       Friday's child is full of woe.
       Saturday's child has far to go.
       And the child that's born on the Sabbath day
       Is bonnie and blithe and good and gay.

2 Working in pairs, or groups of three, the students take the central idea of the poem and reshape it using their own words. Thus, the stem in (a) would be: 'One, two / three, four' etc., and in (b) 'Monday's child is . . .' etc.
3 When they have completed their poems, they exchange them with other pairs.

COMMENTS

1 Traditional rhymes usually rely for their effect on strong rhyme and rhythm. Sense does not always matter!
2 The advantage of using such poems as models is that they can easily be imitated, as the language is usually very simple. And for this reason, such poems can be memorised with little effort. The students should, therefore, be encouraged to read their own versions *aloud*.
3 A possible extension of this exercise is to take the rhythmic pattern of a folk poem or verse in the mother tongue, and find English words to fit the *rhythm*, even if they make little sense.
4 Here is another traditional rhyme:

I Saw a Fishpond

I saw a fishpond all on fire,
I saw a house bow to a squire,
I saw a parson twelve feet high,
I saw a cottage near the sky ...
I saw two sparrows run a race,
I saw two horses making lace,
I saw a girl just like a cat,
I saw a kitten wear a hat,
I saw a man who saw these too,
And said, though strange, they all were true.

(Anon.)

5.10 Haiku

WHAT TO DO

1 Give the students an example of a haiku, such as

> Among the white hairs
> A solitary black one
> Life refuses death.

Explain that the haiku is *always* of the same, fixed form: three lines of five, seven, and five syllables respectively. The lines should preferably *not* rhyme.
2 Now write up several theme words, e.g. snow, computer, spring, compassion. These will be the title words and should not necessarily appear in the poem.
3 Working individually or in pairs, the students now devise haiku of their own, based on one of the theme words. They should read each other's work, comment and criticise. Remember that it is important to keep to the basic structure.

COMMENTS

1 Here, the discussion is almost as important as the writing. Because the haiku encourages compression of thought, the poems will inevitably give rise to questioning and speculation. Time should be allowed for this.
2 A variation on the haiku is the *cinquain*, which is made up of 5 lines of 2, 4, 6, 8 and 2 syllables respectively. Here is an example:

≫→

E

Parting

You leave.
I am left here.
How shall I pass the time –
The days, the long nights, without you?
Tell me.

(A.M.)

3 Another possible variation is one which is made up of 7 lines, of 1, 2, 4, 6, 4, 2 and 1 syllables respectively. Here is an example:

Father to Son

Child –
I see
In your small smile
Reflections of myself,
Happy and young.
I'm old
Now.

(A.M.)

4 If students find tackling a haiku difficult initially, it often helps to provide the first two lines for them, and ask them to find a suitable final line. For example:

I pricked my finger
On these roses you sent me:

Some possible final lines are:
Is this a symbol?
Red is love's colour.
No love without pain.
Did you send the thorn?
Thank you for the thought!

□ See also: Wordshapes (6.5).

5.11 Limericks

WHAT TO DO

1 Ask the students to think of a number of place names – towns or cities
  – and to find at least three words which rhyme with each, for example:
  Pondicherry: merry, berry, ferry, dysentery;
  Rome: home, dome, comb, roam, foam.
2 Give them an example of the limerick-form and ask them to produce
  limericks of their own, following the same rhyme pattern (AABBA).
  Here are some suitable limericks:

> There was an old man in a trunk
> Who enquired of his wife, 'Am I drunk?'
>   She replied with regret
>   'I'm afraid so, my pet',
> And he answered, 'It's just as I thunk.'

(Ogden Nash)

> There was a faith-healer of Deal
> Who said, 'Although pain isn't real,
>   If I sit on a pin
>   And it punctures my skin
> I dislike what I fancy I feel'.

(Unknown)

> There was a young lady of Riga,
> Who went for a ride on a tiger;
>   They returned from the ride
>   With the lady inside,
> And a smile on the face of the tiger.

(Unknown)

COMMENTS

This exercise is not as easy as it looks, and should perhaps be reserved for
a moment when the group seems ready to take on a challenge. On the
other hand the limerick, because it encourages the use of everyday
language, is also a very suitable verse form for foreign learners to imitate.

6 Writing — words

The focus in this chapter is on words: their endings and beginnings, the way they rhyme or resonate, the associations they trigger off. Besides offering another way into the writing of poems, this approach gives valuable opportunities for acquiring and extending vocabulary.

6.1 Word webs

WHAT TO DO

1 Read aloud at slow dictation speed a list of 25–30 words. Students listen but do not write.
2 As soon as you finish ask them individually to write down as many of the words as they can recall.
3 In pairs they compare and amalgamate their lists.
4 Read the list of words again. Students in pairs try to fill in gaps in their combined lists.
5 Pairs then join together to form groups of four. They again amalgamate their lists.
6 Read the list once more. By now most groups will have a more or less complete list.
7 Each group is now asked to put the words they have collected into groups according to association. (Any principle of association may be adopted – by sound, by lexical set, by association etc.)
8 Groups then choose one of their word groupings and work the words into a poem (one word per line).
9 Each group then exchanges its poem with another group. Groups receiving a poem must find two good things about it and make two criticisms of it.
  Here is an example of a possible word list:

sponge	vague	grammar	quiz	water
orange	wheel	hypnotic	shore	white
provoke	cyclone	intolerable	stretch	pyjamas
religion	end	marriage	tent	natural
smelly	gem	physics	trip	manic
moral				
need				

This might generate several sets of associations, for example:
- religion, provoke, marriage, intolerable, moral, need
- natural, wheel, white, manic, hypnotic
- sponge, water, white, shore, natural, smelly

COMMENTS

1   This recall exercise is excellent for involving students in listening care-fully. It also leads to useful and interesting discussion while they are comparing lists. ('She said *manic*?' 'No, *panic*.' etc.) Spelling problems are also highlighted at this stage.
2   One way of connecting this exercise with the more formal parts of the language course is to select words which have recently been encoun-tered in the language course book.
3   An alternative procedure is for each student to write one content-word on a slip of paper. These then form the input to the exercise.
4   The discussion of the language webs is again very important and directs students' attention to the inter-relatedness of words.

□   This exercise may be used in combination with Tangles (2.12) and Rhyme and reason (6.14).

6.2 Drip, drop, drizzle . . .

WHAT TO DO

1   Put up on the blackboard a number of typical initial consonant clusters (e.g. *st-, fl-, spl-, scr-, gr-, fr-, tr-, str-, cr-* etc.).
2   Students work individually. Each one chooses *one* cluster and writes down as many words as possible which start in this way (e.g. *split, splatter, splice, splosh, splash, splay, splat, splutter* etc.).
3   In pairs students exchange their lists and try to add more.
4   Again individually, each works with their original list and groups all the words which seem to belong together (e.g. *splash, splosh, splat, splatter, splutter* – all have to do with the sound of liquid being thrown down in some way).
5   These words are then arranged to form a 'minimalist' poem – one word per line. For example:

Making mudpies for Grandfather

splash,
splosh,
splat.
splatter.
splutter!

6 Students then work in groups of four to compare results. Each member looks at one other person's poem and tries to improve it, either by addition or by re-ordering. Groups then report back to the whole class, reading their most satisfactory efforts. Here is an example:

> ### Building Site Accident
>
> Crevasses,
> Craters,
> Cranes . . .
> Creak,
> Crack!
> Cries,
> Cringe,
> Cringe,
> Crash!
> Crunch!
> . . . Crippled
> Crone –
> Crazy
> Crucifix

COMMENTS

1 This exercise obliges students to forage among their word store, and to re-activate, or discover for the first time, vocabulary items. (It is useful if they have a dictionary to hand so that they can check on items they are unsure of.) It is also a powerful aid to vocabulary acquisition: it has been established that one way we store vocabulary is through matching sound shapes.
2 Through exploring the words which somehow belong together, they are also brought to see how certain sounds have broad semantic family relationships.

□ This exercise may be used in combination with Wordshapes (6.5), Mirror words (6.13) and Rhyme and reason (6.14).

6.3 Opposites

WHAT TO DO

1 Ask the students in pairs to write down as rapidly as possible any words that come to mind, with their opposites: e.g. *thick/thin*, *low/high*, *quick/slow*. These need not necessarily be adjectives. Nouns and verbs,

prepositions etc. can also be used, e.g. *hammer/nail, push/pull, up/down*.

Contrasts by association are also possible e.g. *cat/mouse, fish/net, grindstone/knife*.

2 Each pair should draw up a list of twenty such opposites. Then they look through their list for any rhymes or half-rhymes, e.g. **top**/*bottom*, *go*/**stop**, and finally arrange the words in a short rhyming piece.
3 When the piece is ready they may add further ideas that occur to them while working. They then read out their short poems to other pairs or to the group as a whole.

An example of what might be produced at stage 2 is:

> high, low
> quick, slow
> black, white
> day, night

and at stage 3:

> harmony, strife
> grindstone, knife
> heavy, light
> wrong, right
> loser, winner
> saint, sinner
> death, life
> husband, wife

COMMENTS

1 Even for near beginners, this exercise is easy and enjoyable to do. With more advanced students a useful extension is to 'flesh out' the stark rhymes with linking words. This could produce a poem such as the following:

> I am the *bow*, you are the *arrow*
> You are the *daylight*, I am the *night*
> I am the *wheel*, you are the *barrow*,
> You're never *wrong*, I'm always *right*.
>
> My hair is *silver*, your hair is *gold*
> You like the bed *warm*, I like it *cold*
> I love the *desert*, you love the *sea*
> That's the difference between *you* and *me*.

2 Finally, the students can also be asked to use <u>only</u> the rhyming words from this exercise and work them into a short poem in which no contrasts are required.

6.4 Letters alive

WHAT TO DO

1 Students work in pairs. Each pair chooses one letter of the alphabet to work with. Choice should be based on attraction to its shape (or to its sound).
2 Pairs then write out all the words which they associate with this letter – on the basis of shape or sound or 'feel' (e.g. S – *snake, sinuous, slippery, sexy, slow, slender* etc.).
3 Each pair then joins another pair, preferably one which has been working on the same letter. They share, and explain to each other, their choices. If possible, they compile a joint list.
4 As a group they then use the words from their list to compose a short poem, beginning – '*(the letter) is like* . . . '. For example:

> S is like a snake,
> Slender &
> Slippery &
> Slow.
> Sinuous
> Sinister &
> Sacred.

5 Groups exchange poems. Each group then tries to improve upon the poem it has received.

COMMENTS

1 The different associations thrown up even by something as basic as the shapes of the letters of the alphabet are quite surprising. It is therefore very important that students should explain why they have chosen any given word.
2 It may sometimes be helpful if the poems are accompanied by drawings. For example:

T is like a tying post,
A trigger –
And a tomb.

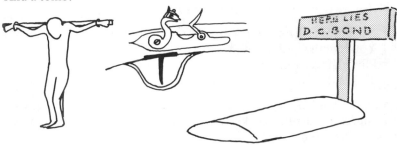

3 One possible variation is to ask students to imagine what one letter might say to another – perhaps a criticism, or a statement of admiration. These could then be formed into a poem. For example:

> S said to T
> 'Loosen up.'
> T said to O
> 'Open out.'
> O said to L
> 'Close up.'
> L said to S
> 'Straighten up.'

□ This exercise may be used in combination with Wordshapes (6.5), Alice's alarming alliteration (6.7), Alphabetically yours (7.1) and ABC (7.2).

6.5 Wordshapes

Examples of the kind of poems suitable for this exercise can be found in collections of 'Concrete Poetry', and in the works of poets such as Guillaume Apollinaire and Edwin Morgan. (The poems or 'wordshapes' need not necessarily be in English.) The two examples below are intended simply as illustrations of the idea.

WHAT TO DO

1 The students work in groups of three. They are asked to draw two or three familiar shapes or patterns, e.g. a ladder, a spiral, a staircase, a pyramid, a conch or shell, a leaf.
2 They then note down as rapidly as possible any words which spring to mind on looking at the shape, e.g.:

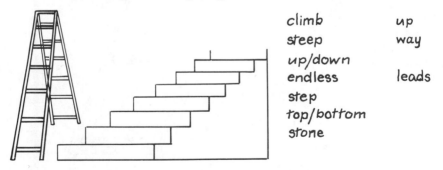

From these words, they select ten to fifteen, and write them down to match the shape they have in mind.

131

3 The groups then compare their wordshapes.

COMMENTS

This exercise is not as easy as it looks. One way of helping the students is to give them the words of a concrete poem or wordshape and ask them to organise them in any pattern they like.

□ See also: Letters alive (6.4) and Mirror words (6.13).
Here are some examples of 'wordshapes':

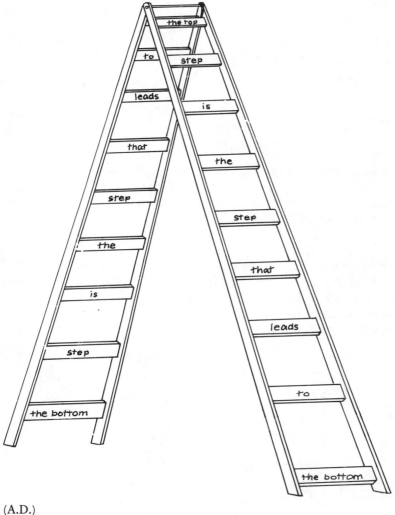

(A.D.)

IF THE ELEPHANT HAD NO TRUNK HOW COULD HE DRINK

?

SNAIL CURL COIL WHORL SHELL SHELL UNCURL FURL COIL WHIRL SHELL COIL WHIRL COIL CURVE SHELTER SHELL ROLL WHORL COIL WHORL SHELL COIL WHORL SNAIL CURL

WHY IS THE HORIZON NOT HORIZONTAL !

(A.D.)

<pre>
                    after- ski

        ski   ski
         ski   ski
          ski   ski
          ski   ski
         ski   ski
        ski   ski
       ski   ski
      ski   ski
     ski   ski
     ski   ski
      ski   ski
       ski   ski
        ski   ski
         ski   ski
          ski   ski
           ski   ski
            ski   ski
             ski   ski
              ski   ski
                ski   ski
                  ski   ski
                    ski   ski
                     ski   ski
                      ski   ski
                       ski   ski
                      ski   ski
                     ski   ski
                    ski   ski
                   ski   ski
                  ski   ski
                 ski   ski
                ski   ski
               ski   ski
              ski   ski
             ski   ski
            ski   ski
           ski   ski
          ski   ski
         ski   ski
        ski   ski
         ski   ski
          ski   ski
           ski   ski
            ski   ski
             ski   ski
              ski   ski
                ski   ski
                 ski ski
                  skiki
                  skisk
                 skis
                ski ski
               ski   ski
               ski   ski
              ski   ski
              ski   ski
             ski ski
              ski
             ski ski
             kisk
             kiss
              kiss
             kiss
</pre>

(A.D.)

6.6 Dictapome

1 Students work in groups of three. Student A dictates a word (any word) to Student B, who writes it down and adds a word of their own. Student B then dictates their two words to Student C, who writes them down, and adds another word. They then dictate their three words to Student A . . . and so on until a complete sentence has been formed. Students should be told at the outset that the results should be a complete sentence.
(e.g. 1   2   3   1   2 3   1
      Trees/and/birds/live/in/the/sun.

2 The process is then repeated until each group has six to eight sentences. These are then arranged in the best order to form a poem. (Some editing can also be done at this stage.)

3 Groups then exchange poems and try to improve on the version they receive. Here is an example of an edited version:

> Trees and birds live in the sun.
> A snake is sleeping silently.
> But the sun is hidden from me –
> I have forgotten my way.
> How far is the nearest star?
> A tree is not good.
> A tree is just a tree.
> A snake is not bad.
> A snake is just a snake.
> Innocence is ignorance.
> I am just me.

COMMENTS

1 We learnt this idea from Mario Rinvolucri (see Paul Davis and Mario Rinvolucri, *Dictation*).

2 Although the students are not usually told to make the sentences relate to each other, they tend to do so naturally.

6.7 Alice's alarming alliteration

1 Give students some examples to show how alliteration (the repetition of the same initial letter in successive words) is used in popular speech, sayings and advertisements. Some of the following could be used:
Big Ben.   As green as grass.
Simple Simon.   A Scotch and Soda.

Wee Willie Winkie.	Better safe than sorry.
As pleased as punch.	A Tiger in your Tank.
As tight as a tick.	Service with a Smile.
As fit as a fiddle.	

2 In pairs they then try to form new sayings using alliteration, on the following model *as . . . as . . .* , for example:
   As temperamental as a taxi driver.
   As pompous as a pope.
   As stiff as a statue.
3 They then compare their efforts in groups of four.
4 Each group is now allotted a certain number of letters from the alphabet (e.g. Group 1 – ABCDE, Group 2 – EFGHI etc.). For each letter the group decides on a line on the *as . . . as . . .* model, like this:
   A – As angry as an actress.
   B – As bored as a boot.
   C – As cold as a cave.
5 In class feedback the contributions from all groups are combined into one alphabet poem.

COMMENTS

1 Alliteration is so widely used both in everyday speech and as a device in poetry that it is well worth alerting students to it early on. Most students enjoy the search for alliterative pairs of words in this activity.
2 If students really get hooked on alliteration they could try this variation: they try to construct sentences on the pattern:
   pronoun + adverb + verb + preposition + adjective + noun
   in which all the words except the pronoun and the preposition are alliterative. Here are some examples:
   – I grimly grapple with grotty grit.
   – I gladly gloat over glamorous glances.
   – I proudly prattle about princely progress.
   – I slowly slide over slippery slopes.
   Because alliteration involves the first letter, students can combine this exercise with the use of a dictionary.

□ See also: Drip, drop, drizzle (6.2).

6.8 The thinginess of things

WHAT TO DO

1 Working in groups of four to six, students choose one word per group from a list of concrete 'things', e.g. *mirror, tunnel, knife, apple, wine, pen, paper, money*, etc.

2 Group members then work individually to write out as many sentences as possible which make 'true' statements about the 'thing' they have chosen. For example:
A mirror is made of glass.
You cannot see through a mirror.
A mirror only looks one way.
Mirrors can be smashed or broken.
It is unlucky to break a mirror.
In a mirror, left is right and right is left.
Not all mirrors are made of glass.
Mirrors were invented long ago.
It is unlucky to look at your lover in a mirror.
People look at mirrors when they are alone.
Mirrors always tell the truth.
Mirrors always lie.
If you break a mirror you will have 7 years bad luck.
Mirrors reflect light.
Mirrors cannot see, they only reflect.
Some mirrors distort reality.
You can use mirrors to see round corners.
Never believe a mirror.

3 Groups then exchange their lists of sentences. They select up to ten of the sentences and arrange them to form a poem. At this stage they may modify or add sentences if it helps to improve the poem.

Here is an example of how the 'raw' ideas might develop into a poem.

> *Money is . . .*
>
> — Paper with pictures nobody looks at
>   Paper with words nobody reads
>
> — The root of all evil . . .
>   the source of all good
>
> — A worry if you have it
>   a worry if you don't
>
> — Something that doesn't grow on trees
> — Freedom

COMMENTS

This exercise allows even very matter-of-fact information about objects to be used as the raw material for poems.

□ This idea may be used in combination with Group poems (7.8).

6.9 As talkative as rain

WHAT TO DO

1 Divide the class into two equal halves. In one group the students work in pairs to produce lists of adjectives — any they can think of (e.g. *talkative, small, bright, jolly, irritable, provoking, spotty, tired*, etc.). In the other group they work in pairs to write out lists of nouns or noun-phrases (e.g. *rain, the sun, a mood, the sea, time, a game, love, fish* etc.).

2 Pairs from one group join with pairs from the other group to form groups of four. Each group now has a list of adjectives and a list of nouns. Students then combine items from the adjective list with those from the noun list, using the structure *as . . . as . . .* (e.g. *as irritable as the sea, as provoking as love, as spotty as a mood, as talkative as rain*, etc.). They should make as many combinations as possible, not just 'normal' ones.

3 Groups then choose combinations which seem to belong together and arrange them in an order they feel looks satisfying as a poem. The poem should then be given a title. Here is an example written using this technique:

As Illogical as Love

As radiant as wine.
As talkative as rain.
As taciturn as a mood.
As indigestible as wood.
As provoking as the wind.
As irritable as the sea.
As casual as tea.
As tight-fitting as a glove —
As illogical as love . . .

And here is one of a similar kind:

Lionel (who is

as lanky as a lampost
as tender as a trap
as loveable as laundry
as subtle as a slap
as popular as purgatory
as handsome as an ape
as cheery as the coldest sneer
as reasonable as rape)

has not been invited
to the annual office party
(because of what happened last year).

(Bernard Young)

COMMENTS

1   The activity can be given sharper focus by using only words which have occurred recently in the course book. These can be displayed in two columns on the blackboard. Students work in pairs combining items from the two columns.
2   One variation is to play the game of consequences in groups of six. Students each write *'as' + an adjective* on a sheet of paper, fold it and pass it to their right-hand neighbour. They all then write *'as' + a noun*, fold the paper, pass it on, write *'as' + an adjective* – and so on until their original paper returns to them. Each person will then have a sheet with three *as . . . as . . .* phrases on it. These are used as input to discussion leading to the poem.

□   This exercise may be used in combination with What I love about . . . (5.6).

6.10 Walk tactfully

WHAT TO DO

1   Divide the class into an even number of about three students per group (six or eight groups is ideal).
2   One half of the groups is asked to work together to produce a list of verbs describing physical actions (e.g. *walk, shout, throw, tickle,* etc.). Set a time limit for this.
3   The other half of the groups writes out a list of adverbs ending in *-ly* (e.g. *quickly, silently, tenderly, cunningly,* etc.). Set a time-limit for this.
4   Each group with lists of verbs then joins a group with lists of adverbs. These new groups of six students each then work to produce *verb + adverb* combinations, drawing upon the lists they have made. As many combinations as possible should be made, without regard for whether they are 'normal' or not. Here is an example of some of the combinations which might emerge: *drink noisily, drop impartially, sing secretively, lift tactfully, bend generously, swim indecently, shout silently,* etc.
5   Each group then chooses up to ten of these *verb + adverb* combinations which might fit together to form a story line, or which other-

⠀⠀⠀»→

wise belong.together. These are arranged in order to form a poem. It is important to choose a clear title. Here is an example:

Song of the Unhappy Wife

Meet casually.
Sing sadly.
Cry courageously.
Shout silently.
Curse callously.
Dance desperately.
Kiss despairingly.
Corner cunningly.
Kill courteously.

COMMENTS

1 Students should be encouraged to look out for the more unusual combinations which often emerge (e.g. *shout silently, smile pessimistically, sing cunningly* etc.), and to discuss possible contexts in which their meanings would become clear and vivid. This often helps in getting them started on a theme for the poem.
2 One possible variation is to ask students to use the *verb + adverb* combinations in full sentences combined into a poem. For example:

They *met casually* at a dance.
She *sang sadly* of romance.

□ This exercise is similar to the *adjective + noun* combinations in 7.3.

6.11 Push over

WHAT TO DO

1 Students work in pairs. They are asked to think of a short incident which could be described solely through phrasal verbs. It may be necessary to give a brief example, for instance:

An Evening's TV Viewing

rush in
switch on
kick off
sit down
nod off
snooze away
wake up
switch off

They should give their poem a title to enable readers to situate it.
2 Each pair then shares its poem with another pair. It should be possible for these minimal poems to be 'read' filling in the missing detail. For example:

> 'Last night I rushed in to catch the football match. I switched on just in time for the kick-off . . . ', etc.

Here is a further example:

Wild West

stride in
pull up
call over
pour out
knock back
pay up
knock back
knock back
fall about
bang into
lash out
knock down
lock up
get away
chase after
round up
shoot down.

COMMENTS

1 Because it requires extensive knowledge of phrasal verbs this activity is only suitable for advanced students.
2 The title is most important, since without it there will be difficulty in knowing how to interpret the list of verbs. It may be useful to point out how important titles often are in poetry. In a sense they alert us to what we should be looking for, and create expectations.
3 It may be helpful to ask groups to write out a 'full' prose version of others' poems as a homework assignment.

□ This exercise is similar to other minimal poem activities. See Dry as dust (6.12) and Tangles (2.12).

6.12 Dry as dust

1   Write a list of concrete nouns on the blackboard, e.g. *sand, steel, tree, mouth, shoe*, etc.
2   Individually students choose one of the words. They then make a list of words they associate with it (e.g. *sand — dry, dusty, desert, dead, gritty, granular, shifting, wind, dunes, oasis, camels* ...). They should be told to start with the physical associations and then widen the associations to memories, experiences, etc.
3   Students then form pairs and exchange their lists. Each one tries to extend his or her partner's list of associations.
4   Pairs then either decide on one list or create a joint list, and try to make a 'word-picture' which sums up the associations it has. Here is an example. It makes use of alliteration — the repetition of the same sounds in the first consonant of each word. Not all the poems can be used to do this.

> *Sand*
>
> gritty
> granular
> grudging
> dust.
> sterile
> shifting
> dead
> dry
> dunes.

1   The exercise can be given sharper focus by selecting words which have recently occurred in the course book.
2   It is important that the exercise is done individually to begin with, since each person's range of associations will be different, even if only slightly so. In the case of *sand* for example, another student might have listed:— *sea, shore, beach, summer, holiday, golden*, etc.
3   One variation is to use the resulting word picture as a chant by continuing to re-combine and permutate it, e.g. *grudging, granular, sterile dunes: gritty, dead, dry dust: shifting, sterile sand: dunes, dead, dry, shifting: sand, granular sand, gritty sand, dead, dry sand,* . . . etc.
4   The exercise can equally well be done using *adjectives* or *verbs* instead of nouns, e.g. *slimy — wet, cold, slippery, nasty*, etc. *shiver — cold, rain, fever, wet, soaked*, etc.

□   This exercise may be used in combination with Letters alive (6.4). The results may be used as a chant. (See 'Sing we and chant it' (4.14).)

6.13 Mirror words

WHAT TO DO

1   Give one or two examples of words which 'mirror' each other in their sound patterns (e.g. *lips–spill*, *peal–leap*, *teach–cheat*, *seal–lease*, *keel–leak*, *tease–seat*, *rule–lure*, etc.).
2   When students have got the idea, ask them to work individually to find as many mirror-pairs as possible.
3   Students then compare their lists in pairs. They note any points of disagreement about sound/spelling correspondences (e.g. *bark–crab*, *not–ton*, *fall–laugh*, etc.) which are then discussed in a full class feedback session. All pairs of words which are agreed are then transferred to the blackboard or OHP.
4   Each student now chooses two pairs of words and writes a sentence for each which contextualises the meanings of the word-pair (e.g. 'You say you *teach* me but you *cheat* me.' 'Your *lips spill* nonsense.' 'I look into your *eyes* and *sigh*.' etc.).
5   Students now work in groups of six. Using the contextualised sentences (and, if they wish, constructing others from the board) they now try to put together a short poem by connecting the meanings of their sentences. Here is one possible example:

> ### Teacher
>
> I look into your *eyes*
> And *sigh* with boredom.
> Your *lips spill* garbage.
> Your *words* are like wet *straw*.
> When you *bark*
> I scuttle like a *crab*
> Into the corner of my *shelf*:
> My *flesh* creeps.
> You try to *lure* me out
> But I will not obey your *rule*.
> Because you *know*,
> You think you *own* me.
> You say you *teach*.
> I say you *cheat*.

6   Groups exchange their poems. Each group then tries to improve upon

the version it has been given. Final versions are discussed in plenary session.

COMMENTS

1 This is useful in concentrating attention on sound/spelling correspondences and the apparent oddities which are revealed in English (e.g. *though–oath, bark–crab*).
2 In discussion there are usually disputed mirror-pairs when students produce metathesis (swapping the order of syllables or consonants) rather than pure mirror-images (e.g. *lips–lisp, cares–scare, nails–snail, words–sword, glass–slag*, etc.). This should be encouraged – and variations like this can be incorporated into the final poem.
3 The sentence contextualisation exercise is usually found helpful for remembering the meanings of new words (e.g. *lure*). In this it is akin to memorisation by antonyms (big–small, etc.). Two words remembered for the price of one!
It is an odd coincidence that these pairs quite often readily suggest a semantic as well as a sound/spelling link (e.g. *keel–leak, seal–lease, spill–lips, tug–gut, eat–tea*, etc.).

□ See also: Drip, drop, drizzle (6.2).

6.14 Rhyme and reason

WHAT TO DO

1 Students work individually. A list of final syllable sounds is put on the blackboard (e.g. *-ink, -ess, -ive, -ie*, etc.). Students choose one sound to work on and make a list of all the one-syllable words which rhyme with this sound (e.g. -ink: *think, link, sink, stink, pink, mink, ink, shrink, kink, wink, blink, prink, drink, slink*, etc.).
2 Each student then tries to choose a set of words from the list which have associative links between them (e.g. *think, drink, link, shrink, kink*).
3 He or she now writes a poem in rhyming couplets using these words as the end-rhymes. For example:

> Psychiatry is a study,
> I always used to *think*,
> Which drove one sane
> And back again to *drink*.

4 Students exchange their poems, even if incomplete, with a partner. Each person now tries to improve upon (or complete) the poem they have received.
5 If there is time, edited versions may be read aloud (or displayed on the class notice-board). Here is an example:

The practice of psychiatry,
I always used to *think*,
Tended to drive one sane
And back again to *drink*.
But now that I myself
Am ironing out a *kink*,
And in despair have taken on
A famous (and expensive) *shrink*.
I fear I must confess I fail
To see the slightest *link*.

COMMENTS

1 In stage 1 students are being obliged to activate their latent vocabulary. It will be useful if they consult a dictionary for words they are in doubt about (e.g. Is there a word *bink*?).
2 In stage 2 it is often useful if students work in pairs, justifying to their partners the links between the words they have chosen. Again a valuable exercise because it forces students to think of words as linked in multiple ways to other words, and not as discrete chunks of meaning.
3 A possible variation is for students to work in groups of five. Each group is given five end-rhymes (e.g. *-in*, *-un*, *-ive*, *-ink*, *-uck*). As a group they find at least five rhyming words for each. (The quickest way of doing this is to assign one rhyme per group member.) The group then chooses the two 'best' rhyming words for each rhyme, keeping in mind that the ten words eventually chosen must have semantic links between them. (They might end up with this: *win/gin*, *gun/fun*, *live/give*, *stink/slink*, *muck/luck*.) The group then uses the words as end-rhymes in a 10-line poem.

□ This exercise may be used in combination with Word webs (6.1) or with Drip, drop, drizzle (6.2).

6.15 Bouts rimés

WHAT TO DO

1 Students work in groups of three.
2 Write on the blackboard a series of rhyming sounds in a rhyme scheme. For example:

-ends   -ins
-oves   -ow
-ends   -ins
-oves   -ow

3 Explain that each group should first of all list as many words which end in this way as possible (e.g. *bends*, *sends*, *lends* . . . ; *loves*, *doves*,

gloves ... ; *wins, tins, pins, begins* ... ; *below, glow, show, go* ... etc.).
4 Groups are then asked to write a poem of two verses following the above rhyme scheme (abab, cdcd) and using some of the words from their lists. For example:

> Every time our kissing ends
> And we put on our hats and gloves,
> Without fail the parting sends
> Us fluttering off like grieving doves.

COMMENTS

This is valuable as a vocabulary consolidation activity. If students have access to a rhyming dictionary, so much the better.

□ This activity can be used in combination with Mirror words (6.13) and Rhyme and reason (6.14).

7 Writing – random association

In this chapter all the techniques depend for their success upon random associations being made between apparently unrelated ideas, objects or words. The techniques are fail-safe. Provided the instructions are followed, something interesting is bound to result. This is not, of course, the end of the story. Whatever is produced has then to be edited, polished and revised in order to be acceptable. But the possibilities of random or chance association as an initial stimulus are enormous.

7.1 Alphabetically yours

WHAT TO DO

1 Students work in groups of four. They prepare a rhyming alphabet using words they know – or in case of need, words they have looked up in the dictionary. Here is an example:

> A is for apple.
> B is for bed.
> C is for chapel.
> D is for dead.
> (etc.)

If possible the poem should rhyme but this is not essential.
2 Groups then exchange their poems. Each group attempts to improve on the version it receives.
3 Each group then reads out its improved version.

COMMENTS

1 This involves students in a motivated search for vocabulary items. The items must fit a given scheme: the first letter must be right, the number of syllables must be right to fit the rhythm, and the sound must be right in order for it to rhyme.
2 One variation is to increase the complexity of the basic structure of each line, like this for example:

>>>→

> A is for apple, which lies in the grass.
> B is for beer, which froths in the glass.
> C is for curry, which we love to eat.
> D is for dumplings, which are a real treat.
> etc.

3 There are any variations which can be worked on this idea. The gram-matical pattern may be varied (as in 2), the vocabulary items can all be drawn from one area of association (sport, food, music etc.), the names of class members and their characteristics can be chosen, for example:

> A is for Alan, with his nose in a book,
> B is for Barry, who likes a good look.
> (etc.)

□ This exercise may be used in combination with Letters alive (6.4) and ABC (7.2).

7.2 ABC

WHAT TO DO

1 Students work in groups of four. They write down together a list of first names beginning with A, then with B, then C etc. (e.g. *Alex, Andrew, Alan, Abraham*, etc.; *Brian, Ben, Beatrice, Brenda*, etc.). They should write out as many names as possible for each letter.
2 They then prepare a rhythmic chant poem based on these names. For example:

> Alex, Brenda, Charles and Doris,
> Esther, Freddy, George and Harold,
> Ivor, Josie, Keith and Lily,
> Mary, Naomi, Olive and Peter,
> Quintin, Roger, Sue and Tricia,
> Ugo, Victor, Will and Xavier,
> Yasmin and Zacharia!

3 Each group then performs its chant.

COMMENTS

1 The main object is to get students to develop a feel for rhythm, using familiar material.
2 A possible variation is to ask them to produce three (or four) names per line, each beginning with the same letter. For example:

> Andrew, Adrian and Alfred,
> Brian, Briony and Bertrand.
> Carol, Cedric and Charley.

3 Instead of personal names, the names of cities, or countries, or animals, or flowers or food – or almost anything, may be used.

☐ This exercise may be used in combination with Letters alive (6.4) and Alphabetically yours (7.1).

7.3 Consequences

WHAT TO DO

1 Collect from the class examples of uncountable 'abstract' nouns (e.g. *life*, *hope*, *trouble*, *time*, *anger*, etc.). List them on the blackboard. You need about fifteen to twenty words.
2 Do the same for uncountable 'concrete' nouns (e.g. *water*, *stone*, *tea*, *bread*, *money*, etc.). You again need fifteen to twenty words.
3 Students work in pairs. Each one writes a question in the form 'What is ....?', completing the blank with a word taken from *one* of the lists on the board (e.g. What is *life*?). It is important only to use one of the lists. The student then folds the paper so that their partner cannot see it and passes it to them.
4 On receiving the paper each one then writes an answer of the form: 'It's ....' The blank must be filled by an adjective which involves a value-judgement (e.g. It's *appalling*. It's *indecent*. It's *stupid*. It's *over-rated*. etc.).
5 Students repeat this four times. They now have four question/answers each. These are unfolded and read together. They then choose the four most striking (or bizarre) results and combine them into a short poem. Here is an example:

> What is bread?
> It's boring.
> What is water?
> It's stupid.
> What is sand?
> It's deceitful.
> What is stone?
> It's sincere.

COMMENTS

1 At first sight this might seem a pointless and irrational exercise. However the results are often striking, even though they are achieved through random means. One of the language-learning spin-offs is the discussion generated when *choosing* the four items. It may be necessary to ensure that students discuss the plausibility of the new combinations. For instance, in what sense is it true that water is stupid, or

sand deceitful or stone sincere? This activity can generate very lively discussion (e.g. Sand is deceitful because it does not stay in one place for long, it changes its shape, it looks like gold but isn't, etc.).

2 This exercise type allows for almost infinite variation:

Why does ....?
Because ....

I love ....ing.
That's because you're .... (adjective)

When I was young I used to .... (verb)
But now I only ....

☐ This exercise can also be used in combination with Serious consequences (7.4).

7.4 Serious consequences

WHAT TO DO

1 Students work in groups of six. Each one is given a sheet with an identical line written on it. (Ideally this should be the first line of a real poem.) He or she then writes a line which follows on from this line, and passes their paper to their right-hand neighbour.
2 Each student now has two lines of poetry. They write a third, which fits in with the first two. They then fold the paper so that only the last line is visible and pass it to their right-hand neighbour.
3 Each student now writes a line which fits the one line they can see, folds the paper so that only the last line is visible and passes it to their right-hand neighbour. This process continues until the papers have returned to their starting points.
4 Each student now unfolds the paper and reads the seven-line poem they find there.
5 The poems are shared and the group decides which is the most satisfactory. If necessary, minor changes can be made to improve it (perhaps by making the text more coherent as discourse).
6 The poems are then presented to the class. Here are two examples:

a)   Remember me when I am dead.
     Keep my picture in your head.
     Let absence make your heart grow fonder,
     As it will make mine.
     I do not see a meaning.
     But perhaps there is some sense
     That we may see when time relents.

b) Who knows why the wind blows?
    Who knows why the birds sing?
    Why stars shine and disappear, clouds gather, lightning strikes?
    I am confused, amazed, surprised.
    It's neither confusing, nor amazing, nor surprising.
    Still I wonder how it happened.
    Do not wonder: rejoice it happened.
    Ask no questions – just rejoice.

COMMENTS

1 The results of the exercise will usually be rather imperfect, rough-hewn versions. But this is in itself an advantage, since it gives the opportunity for discussion and re-drafting of improved versions. Such discussion will often focus on cohesive features between one line and another, or on the overall pattern of meaning within the poem. Factors such as rhyme and rhythm will also often arise.
2 An alternative procedure is to allow students to see the *two* preceding lines rather than only one. This makes it easier to maintain coherence/cohesion.
3 Alternatively the growing poem can be circulated with no folding. In this way each student can see everything written so far, and simply has to add his or her line.

☐ This exercise can be used as a development of Consequences (7.3).

7.5 Acrostics

WHAT TO DO

Write a single word vertically on the blackboard, for example:

C   W
O   H
N   I
F   S
L   P
I   E
C   R
T

Each letter marks the beginning of a line.

Working alone, or in pairs, the students now produce a short poem based on the stimulus word. For instance:

⫸→

a)   Constantly quarrelling
        Over small things of
        No importance.
        Fraying the edges of our
        Lives with nagging.
        Impotent rage poisons us,
        Critical and cantankerous,
        Till death takes us away.

b)   Why do people in public places
        Have to lower their voices?
        Is it because they fear
        Someone might overhear?
        Perhaps . . . But why do they bother?
        Every word they try to conceal
        Reaches us loud and clear.

When finished, the students compare their results.

COMMENTS

1 The framework serves both as a constraint and as a stimulus. This exercise will work best if a fairly strict time-limit (5–7 mins.) is set, as this will encourage the students to put down the lines without too much reflection.
2 Other enjoyable variants include:
        the use of proper nouns and names, e.g. AMAZON, SIGMUND FREUD, VIVALDI, HONOLULU . . . ;
   –   familiar, everyday words, such as: POST OFFICE, HEADACHE, BREAKFAST, TIMETABLE.

7.6 Peace–dove–crow–black . . .

WHAT TO DO

1 Students work in groups of three. In each group one student acts as secretary and notes down the words the other two use when playing the word association game.
2 The other two students begin to play the game: they take it in turns to provide a word which is associated with the one immediately preceding it (e.g. *stone – wall – house – room – space – stars – comet – burn up – rubbish – waste – time – clock – watch – look – eyes – blue – bird – feather – bed*, etc.). This should go on until the secretary has noted down about 25–30 words.
3 All three members of the group now select, individually, up to ten words which seem to them to belong together somehow. Then they

write a poem around them. (There is no need for these words to come at the ends of lines, so long as they are incorporated into the poem in some way.) Here is an example (words chosen underlined):

> I gaze into the <u>mirror</u> on the <u>wall</u>:
> <u>Images</u> flicker, weave and merge.
> I look and see my mother
> When she was forty,
> And her <u>bones</u> were drying.
> <u>Ghosts</u> creep on to me from musty <u>corners</u>,
> Mammoth lurking shadows, whispering <u>fear</u>.
> Invisible hands grab for me from the <u>floor</u>.
> I try hiding in the attic.
> I hear little feet <u>stamp</u> up the stairs.
> In my veins my blood is a colourless fluid,
> Odourless, tasteless and congealed like <u>gum</u>.
> Growing old is dying slowly.

4 Students in each group then swap poems, attempt to improve them and discuss the results.

COMMENTS

1 The word association game itself offers good opportunities for careful listening and recall.
2 The discussion of each other's work may be focused on:
   – the choice of words
   – the way they have been woven into the finished product
   – the suggested improvements (by introducing rhyme, by changing the breaks between lines etc.).

☐ This exercise may be used in combination with Word webs (6.1) and Keywords I (8.10).

7.7 A sweeping nose and a running statement

WHAT TO DO

1 Students are asked individually to compile lists of common *adjective + noun* phrases (e.g. *football match, a dance hall, a running nose, a sweeping statement, a heavy cold, a common problem*, etc.). Each person should write at least twelve such phrases.
2 Again individually students then re-combine the adjectives with other nouns (e.g. *a heavy hall, a sweeping nose, a dance statement, a running problem*, etc.).

3 In pairs, students exchange their lists of these new combinations, and choose those which seem to be especially striking or unusual (e.g. *a sweeping nose, a dance match, a football cold,* etc.). Only really good combinations should be used.
4 Pairs then discuss these new combinations and try to explain to each other what they might mean in as plausible a way as possible. It may sometimes be helpful to draw a picture to aid the explanation!
5 Each pair then arranges the striking combinations they have chosen to form a short poem. They should also agree on a title which will clarify the poem and help others to give it a particular meaning. Here is an example:

> *Old Age*
>
> an evil knee
> a razor's cough
> a wheezing edge
> a whistling head
> a wounded kettle
> a severed eye
> a mouldy engine
> a rotten nail
> a rusty tooth
> a spongy door
> a creaking cake
> a leaking smell
> a musty tap
> a puffing bag

6 Each pair then joins another to form groups of four. Poems are exchanged: two good points are to be found, and two weak ones.

COMMENTS

1 This 'hands-on' working with language helps to remove the students' worry about 'making mistakes'. It also helps to refine their sensitivity to what is an acceptable or striking combination. The unusual nature of the results obliges them to look at familiar words in an unfamiliar way and to discover meaning potentials they will often not have realised were there.
2 A possible variation is to allow combinations in both directions. For example:

> a common problem
> a dance hall

could become:

a common hall
a dance problem

or:

a problem hall
a problem dance
a common dance
(etc.)

3 If a close link with the language course book is desirable, the *adjective + noun* phrases can be taken direct from texts in units recently covered.

☐ This exercise may be used in combination with Alternative words (2.3).

7.8 Group poems

WHAT TO DO

1 Students work in groups of eight. Distribute to each group a theme word. This should be the property of the group and not communicated to other groups (e.g. *horses, milk, hate, nightmares, parting, sleep, fog,* etc.).
2 Each person in the group writes out, individually, one short sentence which crystallises their feelings about the theme word (e.g. *Fog is the weather for dark secrets*).
3 The group's contributions are then collected and exchanged with another group's. So – each group finds itself with eight sentences written on a single theme from another group. These sentences are then to be arranged in the best order, with some minimal editing, if necessary, to form a poem. Here is an example:

Unedited version

The fog sits on our town like a suffocating blanket.
Fog snarls up the traffic.
Fog stops the trains and keeps the planes on the ground.
Fog makes us keep the lights on even at noon.
Fog gets inside my head and stops me thinking.
I hate the way fog chokes me.
When the fog comes, old people choke to death.
Fog is the weather for dark secrets.

Edited version

The fog smothers our town like a suffocating blanket,
Snarling up the traffic,
Stopping the trains,

155

F

Grounding the planes.
(Old people choke to death.)
It makes us fight for breath:
We keep lights burning even at noon.
It even gets inside my head,
Confuses my thoughts.
Outside night is mixed with day
In a timeless grey.
Anything could happen.
Fog is the weather for dark secrets.

COMMENTS

1 Since each group 'inherits' its raw material from another group, it is easier to change and edit the sentences: no one is personally attached to a particular verbal formation.
2 The exercise involves discussion of the best *order* for the ideas, and of the best *form* for them to be expressed. Factors such as connectivity, rhyme and rhythm will all crop up quite naturally in this connection.
3 This activity can be given sharper focus by choosing the stimulus words from semantic areas covered recently in the course book (e.g. types of food, transport, weather, clothing, etc.), or by using proper names which are topical at the time.

7.9 Computer poems

WHAT TO DO

1 Demonstrate on the blackboard how a single sentence can be permutated, using the same words to produce a series of different sentences. For example:

Nobody knows the woman he loves.
He loves the woman nobody knows.
He knows the woman nobody loves.
The woman nobody knows he loves.
The woman nobody loves he knows.
The woman he loves knows nobody.
Nobody loves the woman he knows.
Nobody he knows loves the woman.
Nobody he loves knows the woman.
The woman loves nobody he knows.
The woman knows nobody he loves.

(A.M.)

After putting up the first couple of sentences, elicit others from the students.

2 Write up the following sentences for consideration:
 – Who knows why the wind blows?
 – Everyone gets what he deserves.
 – Nothing is ever for ever.
 – Do you know how much you mean to me?
 – This thing we have I like.

3 Students work individually. Each one chooses a sentence and tries to find as many combinations as possible of the words it contains. (At this stage *no* changes are allowed.)

4 Students then compare their lists of sentences in pairs, and check that no other sentences are possible.

5 Then, still in pairs, they try to agree on the most effective ordering of these sentences to make a poem.

6 Each pair then joins another to form groups of four. Poems are exchanged and evaluated, and proposals for improvements made.

COMMENTS

1 It is not easy to find sentences which allow of recombination in this way. It is worth brainstorming with colleagues to develop a list of such sentences.

2 This is a very valuable exercise for stretching the students' syntactic sensitivity. How much will the language bear? What are the limits to syntactic variation? (e.g. Is 'Everyone he deserves gets what?' acceptable?)

3 After the first attempt, which may lead to frustration and failure, it is sometimes helpful to allow for minimal variation in the words of the original sentence. (e.g. Do *you* know how much *you* mean to me? 'You' or 'I' may be used. So sentences such as 'Do *I* know how much *you* mean to me?' become possible.)

□ This exercise may be used in combination with Jumbled lines (2.5), Tangles (2.12) and A little goes a long way (8.1).

7.10 The referee on the roof

WHAT TO DO

1 Students begin by working individually. They will need a dictionary each. They open the dictionary at random, and write down the first noun which strikes their eye on the pages in front of them. They repeat the process. Each student should now have two nouns (e.g. *buffalo/ faith-healer, liver/molehill, referee/roof, stick/temple, vein/tulip*).

2 Students repeat the process three times, so that each one has three pairs of words.
3 They now form groups of three and share the words they have collected. They should try to discover possible links between the words in any pair. For example, what might the connection be between a referee and a roof? (Perhaps he has been chased there by irate football fans.)
4 They then choose the pair of words which seem to have the most interesting (or bizarre) connection and compose a short poem together to bring out the connection. Here is an example:

> The referee climbed onto the roof
> And sat there all alone.
> The referee had made a goof
> And the fans made him atone.

COMMENTS

1 The random nature of the search will always throw up interesting new vocabulary items, which will usually be retained because of the unusual way in which they are encountered.
2 A sharper focus can be given to the exercise if nouns recently encountered in the course book are used. In this case students would draw slips with the words written on them from a box. This procedure however is unlikely to produce such fertile associations as a completely random procedure.
3 One possible variation is to ask the students in any one group to write a poem incorporating all the pairs of words they have produced (e.g. a poem combining *orange/pacifism, liver/molehill, referee/roof, spine/ state, vein/tulip, howitzer/idea, poison/temple, shadow/shirt, hill/ clock*).
4 Another variation is to ask each group to find six words by using the same random dictionary procedure. These six words have then to be linked by association, and used in a short poem.

7.11 The clutches of the cliché

WHAT TO DO

1 Students work in groups of four. Distribute a tourist brochure to each group.
2 Each group then selects from its brochure, and lists, the most obvious clichés (e.g. *golden beaches, palm-fringed lagoons, star-lit evenings, a welcome you'll remember*, etc.).
3 These are then arranged into a cliché poem. When deciding on an order for each item, the groups should keep in mind the rhythm of the poem. It should be possible to read out the poem as a chant.

4 Each group then prepares its chant for performance to the other groups.

COMMENTS

1 There are many sources for the cliché: political (and other) speeches, sports reports, book reviews, advertising copy, etc. ('Pseuds' corner' in *Private Eye* is an excellent source.) Here is an example of a poem using clichés from introductory speeches.

> ### Does he mean me?
>
> Just a few words
> Auspicious occasion.
> Honoured to receive
> Credit to the nation
> Very pleasant duty
> Before taking my leave
> Lover of truth and beauty
> If I did not say
> Man of many parts
> Brilliant researcher in every way
> Not only science but also the arts
> Left a profound impression
> Distinguished guest
> Widely respected in the profession
> Laboured without rest
> Must not omit to mention
> Long list of publications
> Bring to your kind attention
> Well-deserved decorations
> Appointed to present post
> Conducted his investigations
> Deserved it more than most
> Exemplary attitude
> Heartfelt gratitude.
> Needs no introduction from me . . .
>
> (A.M.)

2 Stages 2 and 3 above lead students to examine the language carefully before they decide what is cliché and what to include. It will also involve them in discussion on the best order – keeping the rhythmic criterion in mind.

3 This writing task can form the *preparation* stage for certain types of poem (e.g. e. e. cummings' *next to of course god america i* . . .).

7.12 **Prose into poem**

1 Choose one or more short prose passages which could be written out
as poems. Here is an example:

> Each thing that goes away returns and
> nothing in the end is lost. The great friend
> throws all things apart and brings all things
> together again. This is the way everything
> goes and turns round. That is how all living
> things come back after long absences, and in
> the whole great world all things are living
> things. All that goes returns. He will return.
>
> How can I not know it when all my years I
> have watched the sun go down times
> unending toward the night only to come again
> from the dawn the opposite way? Too true, it
> is so long since I last saw the sun, going or
> coming. But my skin continues to tell the heat
> from the cold, and I know it is I who have
> changed, not the changing circle of the world
> itself. And yet even here things have come
> about lately to put me into more fearful
> doubts than my tired soul can hold. Have two
> nights passed? Or is it two whole weeks that
> have passed me by?

> (Ayi Kwei Armah, *Fragments*)

2 Students work individually to write this out as a poem. This will
involve them in deciding on where the boundary between one line and
another should come to obtain the best effect. For example:

> Each thing that goes away
> Returns
> And nothing in the end
> Is lost.

or

> Each thing
> That goes away
> Returns
> And nothing
> In the end
> Is lost.

3 When they have finished, they compare and discuss their versions.

COMMENTS

1 This exercise highlights the way in which we are conditioned by the visual layout of what we read. This will influence the way we read it. Indeed one way of demonstrating this is to ask students to exchange their 'poems' and then to read aloud the version they have been given. How does the break up into lines affect the reading?
2 It will be important in the discussion to examine to what extent rhythm has influenced the way the lines have been broken up.

□ This exercise may be used as a direct follow up to Poetry or prose? (2.1).

8 Writing – from experience

In this chapter we focus upon the students' own sensations, experiences and ideas as the source of poems. The variety of ideas and techniques drawing on this source is virtually inexhaustible. Only a few sample techniques are set out in full. Others have been outlined in the final section.

8.1 A little goes a long way

WHAT TO DO

1 Students work individually. Each one is asked to write down the ten words which they think are most important for communicating in English. Only ten words are permitted (e.g. *I, you, yes, no, good, please, give, have, do, speak, ask*).

2 In groups of four, they then try to have 'conversations' using only their *own* set of ten words. However difficult this is found to be, they should persist until all the possible sentences have been formed and used several times.

3 Working individually again, they add six new words to their lists. They may also discard and replace up to four of the words from their original list. A new list might look something like this:

old	replacement	new
you	not	we
good	like	me
have	come	us
do	go	to
speak		what

4 In the same groups they again try to have conversations using their *own* lists only.

5 Individually again they are asked to add eight new words. They may again discard and replace four of the words from the previous list.

6 In the same groups they again try out their words in conversations.

7 Individually, they use some or all of their words (but no others) to compose a short poem. Here is an example using only fifteen words:

162

This thing we have I like.
It is good.
I like it.
You like it.
We like it.
What is this thing?
What is this thing we like?
I do it.
You do it.
We do it.
We like it.
It is good.
There is nothing like it!

8   Within each group students read out and compare their poems. Where possible they suggest improvements in each other's work.

COMMENTS

1   In a sense this is a creative extension of a Silent Way technique, where students are encouraged to make the maximum use of minimum resources. This obliges them both to extract the last drop of meaning from their words through syntactic juggling, and to think very carefully about which new words to choose and discard. A kind of linguistic poker in fact! It also makes them listen very carefully to the words others in their group are using, since this is one very good source of new words for their own lists.

2   One variation is to prepare a number of slips of paper with words written on them (enough for each group to take fifteen to twenty each). The words should be composed of function words (in multiple copies) plus content words which have recently occurred in the text-book. The slips are jumbled and placed in a box. Each group then draws fifteen to twenty slips and uses the words they contain to form a minimal language poem.

☐   This exercise may be used in combination with Tangles (2.12), Group poems (7.8) and Computer poems (7.9).

8.2 That old refrain . . .

WHAT TO DO

1   Explain the function of refrains in some types of poetry (e.g. ballads). Generally the refrain repeats the underlying message of the poem, and this repetition serves to reinforce the message. Here is an example from a well-known ballad.

It's the same the whole world over,
It's the poor that get the blame.
It's the rich that get the pleasure,
And it's all a crying shame.

2   Students work in groups of four. Each group decides upon a theme, which may be born from almost any simple observation (e.g. *It always happens to me* or *Who cares?* or *Why is the weather always wet?* or *Some days I feel happy.* etc.).

3   They then try to write a four-line verse which will act as a refrain in a longer poem. For example:

(a)   It always happens to me –
      Never to the others.
      It always happens to me –
      But no one ever bothers.

(b)   Who cares?
      What can I do?
      No one cares –
      Or only a few.

(c)   Now's the time for action.
      Now's the time to act.
      Forget about your fiction
      And face up to hard fact.

(d)   Why is the weather always wet?
      Why is it always cold?
      I don't know whether the weather
      Will improve before I'm old.

4   Each group then writes a poem which begins and ends with the refrain, and has three verses with repetitions of the refrain in between, e.g. Verse 1 refrain, *Verse 2*, Verse 3 refrain, *Verse 4*, Verse 5 refrain, *Verse 6*, Verse 7 refrain. Usually these intermediate verses will tell a story, or give concrete details of the theme which the refrain outlines. Here is an example:

Africa

Refrain   Who cares?
            What can I do?
            No one cares –
            Or only a few.

> There's millions are sickly
> And millions starving –
> Yet there's not a soul
> Will do anything.

Refrain   Who cares? . . .

> Those sickness and hunger
> Do not liquidate,
> Are soon taken care of
> By communal hate.

Refrain   Who cares? . . .

> Though Live Aid and Sport Aid
> Have raised a few bob,
> The United Nations
> Ain't doing its job!

Refrain   Who cares? . . .

COMMENTS

1 The results of this activity are usually ideal for oral expression work because refrains are made for speaking aloud (see chapter 4). In the example given above, the refrain might be read aloud by the whole class, and each verse (or each couplet of the other verses) could be read by individuals.
2 This is an activity which can usefully be done as a homework assignment. Once the refrain itself has been decided upon, group members agree to bring back their verses to the next lesson, when they are discussed and the best chosen.

8.3 Colours I

WHAT TO DO

1 Choose a colour – one only – and write it on the board: e.g. *yellow*.
2 Each student writes down, as fast as possible, any spontaneous associations the word arouses, no matter how 'obvious' they may be. This should take no more than two to three minutes.
3 In pairs, the students compare and expand their lists. They then select whichever ideas appeal to them most and develop them into a poem which will take its shape from the material they have produced. Here is a fairly simple example:

⟫→

Yellow

sunflower, cowardice, quarantine
a river in China, a submarine
   moon, sun, desert sand
   the long road to Samarkand
mustard, custard, Cheddar cheese
pages in telephone directories
Olympic medals, haloes on saints
advertisements for industrial paints
the kitchen – before we painted it white
the colour of the dress I wore last night.

(Workshop)

COMMENTS

In this exercise, as in the previous one, we are drawing on the personal experiences of each member of the group. What we have proposed here is merely the first stage in the development of themes which might lead to more ambitious work.

8.4 Colours II

WHAT TO DO

1 Divide the students into groups of six. In each group the students choose one colour per group member.
2 Each student, individually, writes out as many phrases as possible on the *as ... as ...* pattern. These phrases should convey a vivid impression of his or her colour e.g. *as grey as a Sunday, as green as a card table.*
3 Group members then share their items. They agree on one item per colour which they think is most striking. The six items are then combined into a chart, by permutating the order of the items. Here is an example:

   As black as cherries
   As blue as veins
   As red as berries
   As grey as brains
   As green as creme-de-menthe
   As yellow as my old aunt

COMMENTS

1 One of the objects is to break the stranglehold of clichéd comparisons (e.g. *as black as ink*). It is therefore worth spending some time on class

discussion of the more lively items thrown up by the exercise, e.g. Which is the most striking comparison in the above poem? Which the most/least expected?

2 An alternative is to ask all the members of a given group to produce items for a single colour, e.g. *as black as sheep*, *as black as mountain roots*.

3 Other base structures could also be used, e.g. Redd**er than** . . . , Not so red *as* . . . etc.

8.5 Smells

WHAT TO DO

1 As a warming-up exercise, the students think of a familiar smell and a *place* or *time* associated with that smell, e.g. the smell of mothballs in cupboards, the smell of boiled milk at breakfast.

2 Working in pairs, they combine their lists and then organise the lines in a rhythmic pattern. No rhymes are needed.

3 When ready, they compare their work with that of another pair and together devise a short piece made up of the best lines. For instance:

Smells of . . .

> athletes in changing-rooms
> magazines in waiting-rooms
> chlorine in swimming-baths
> stale breath in telephone-booths
>
> > cheap scent in fitting-rooms
> > maiden aunts in sitting-rooms
> > cabbage in college dining-halls
> > incense in Catholic cathedrals
> > wet dogs on dirty mats
> > pampered cats in airless flats
> > acid in pipettes
> > salami in couchettes
> >   and
> > toothpaste on a lover's breath.

(Workshop)

COMMENTS

1 It is best not to give the students a model to follow, as this may inhibit their work. Rather, allow them to develop the poem in their own way so that they feel free to choose their own rhythm and length of line.

2 A variant on this theme is: 'The smell of .... reminds me of
   ....'
3 The same exercise may also be done with tastes and sounds.

8.6 Fast reflexes

WHAT TO DO

1 Students work in groups of four. Each group is given a different picture
   in a sealed envelope. When you give the word, they open the envelope,
   look at the picture and *immediately* each student writes his/her
   reactions in a few sentences in prose. (It may be helpful to specify that
   they should frame their reactions as a) questions b) feelings/sensa-
   tions.)
2 Within each group, students compare their reactions and prepare a
   'group reaction' written on a single sheet of paper.
3 Groups then exchange their pictures and reactions sheet. As a group,
   they then work on the prose material and transform it into a poem on
   the picture. (They may decide to leave out some of the material and to
   substitute new ideas of their own.)
4 Groups then return their poems to the originating groups. These now
   edit and improve the poem they receive, if possible. Here is an example:

Special Delivery

What can it be?
Is it for me?
Is it a bill?
Or a 'billet doux'?
Or a belated birthday card?
A letter from the bank manager?
A delivery by special messenger?
An invitation to a dance?
The start of a romance?
The end of an affair?
And do I dare
To open
It?

COMMENTS

1 It is important that the initial prose reaction is rapid. Immediate reactions are more likely to throw up interesting ideas.
2 The opportunities for language work are many: in the discussion and drafting of the group prose version, in the selection of items for inclusion in the poem, ordering them and deciding on additions etc.

☐ See also Everyday things (3.3, 4), Visualisation (2.8).

8.7 Notice how . . .

WHAT TO DO

1 Students are given a picture to look at in detail (see p. 170).
2 Individually they note down all the details they can observe (e.g. a corpse is lying in a coffin in the centre foreground. In the background a man is hanging from the gallows).
3 In pairs they compare notes and fill in any details they may have missed.
4 Pairs join together to form groups of four. Each group decides upon eight salient details. Group members then write these into a poem. It will often be helpful to use sentences which draw the reader's attention to what is going on (e.g. Notice how . . . See how . . . etc.). And to formulate questions which might form in the mind of someone looking at the picture (e.g. And is this everybody's fate? Is there no pity? This could be worked into a refrain. Compare 'I must die/God have mercy upon us' etc.).
5 Groups exchange their poems and try to improve the version they receive.

COMMENTS

1 Clearly it is important to choose a picture which contains plenty of action or detail (e.g. Goya's The 3rd of May 1808, Le Nain's The Peasant Family, Delacroix's Liberty Guiding the People, Velazquez's The Surrender of Breda, etc.). The exercise can however equally well be applied to portraits (Rembrandt, Dürer and the Holbeins provide rich resources). In this case however attention has to be focused on speculation about the character of the person portrayed, and the kind of life and events he or she has experienced.

2 An alternative way of using the picture is to decide upon a new title for it (e.g. Mortality). Then to use the title to write an acrostic (where each

letter of the title forms the first letter of the first word in each line of the poem). See Acrostics (7.5).

☐ See also Illustration (2.9), Contrasts III (2.16). A good source of poems and pictures is 'Voices in the Gallery', ed. Dannie and Joan Abse.

8.8 To your face and behind your back

WHAT TO DO

1 Students work individually. Everyone has experienced situations where we say things but we are not necessarily sincere. We may be thinking something quite different from what we say! (e.g. You go to a party and see someone you don't like. You say 'How nice to see you again' but what you think is 'Oh my God. Not him!'). Students then rule two columns on a sheet of paper. In one column they write what they *say* in a given situation. In the other they write what they *think* while they are saying it. Each student should produce at least 3 examples.
2 In pairs students compare what they have written, and try to add further examples.
3 They then work to arrange their examples in the best order to form a poem. Here is an example:

To your face	*Behind your back*
How kind of you to let me come.	I'd rather die than visit that bum.
Your cheeks are cherry, Your eyes honey.	Don't mind it, It's just baloney.
Thanks awfully, You saved my life.	I wouldn't be surprised If you stuck me with a knife.
Isn't it hot?	That's it, now I'm caught.
Will it rain tonight?	Not that I care even if it might.

(Workshop)

COMMENTS

1 One possible variation is to ask students to think of a situation in which they did not perform particularly well (e.g. they lost an argument, agreed to do something they did not want to do etc.). They then rule two columns: What I said/What I wish I had said. They then follow the same procedure as above.

2 Another variation is 'Broken Promises'. We have all had experiences when another person has failed to keep a promise. Students note down three such instances from their own experience, and use these as the basis for a poem, e.g. She said she'd write but no letter ever came. He said he'd call but the phone stayed silent. etc.

3 Students can work in pairs to speak aloud poems like this. One student (or group) speaks 'To your face', the other 'Behind your back'.

□ See Themes: conversation (3.5) and In character (4.9).

8.9 From pictures into words

WHAT TO DO

1 Present a picture which will spark off reactions and ideas without necessarily being too explicit. Here is one example:

2 Individually students write down *one* sentence which the picture suggests to them (e.g. *It's his fault, not mine. I'm not the one to blame. It's not my job. Why don't you ask him over there?* etc.).

3 Working in groups of six, students now combine their sentences into a short poem which will somehow summarise the message or the effect of the picture. They should also provide a title. They may, if they wish, add lines and edit their sentences at this stage. Here is an example:

The Responsibility II

The responsibility, my dear sir, lies elsewhere
It is beyond our control.
There is nothing I can do to help.

Not me – him.
Not us – them.
You need something? Why ask me?
Something wrong? Why ask us?
It's him, it's them you need.

There must be a mistake.
It's not my fault.
I was given instructions – by him.
Wrong department –
Try over there.
Please use the proper channels.
My orders came from above.
I can't help.
Sorry.
The responsibility, dear lady, always lies elsewhere
Things have long been beyond our control.

I cannot even help myself.

4 Groups exchange their finished poems, and try to improve on the one
they receive. Final versions can then be read out or displayed.

COMMENTS

Here are some other pictures which have worked well:

☐ See also Using pictures (1.1) and Visualisation (2.8).

8.10 Keywords I

WHAT TO DO

1 Choose a prose text which is relatively rich in 'strong' or emotive content words. Here is an example.

> About the same hour, Voss went to the mouth of the cave. If he was shivering, in spite of the grey blanket in which he had prudently wrapped himself, it was not through diffidence, but because each morning is, like the creative act, the first. So he cracked his finger-joints, and waited. The rain was withdrawn.
>
> (Patrick White, from *Voss*)

2 Students work individually on the text and extract from it what each considers to be 'key' words (e.g. *hour, mouth, cave, shivering, grey blanket, morning, creative, act, cracked, waited*).

3 They then write a short poem in which these words again figure as key words. They should not consult the prose passage again. Neither is it necessary to 're-tell' the story of the prose passage. The words alone should be allowed to suggest new associations. Here is an example:

In the hour before morning,
I stood in the mouth
of the cave,
Waited,
Shivering,
In the grey blanket
Of the dawning
For the original creative act –
Waited till the sky cracked –
To let in the day.

4 Students exchange their work with a partner and try to improve upon what they are given. They then discuss their suggested improvements in pairs.

COMMENTS

1 The initial activity of choosing key words is in itself useful in that it focuses attention on the way these words give a passage thematic unity and colour.
2 Not all students will choose the same set of words, and they will certainly write different poems. This provides fuel for discussion in stage 4 when students exchange their poems and suggest improvements.
3 One possible variation is to give different texts to each student. When the key words have been chosen each student passes their set to a neighbour who then writes the poem based on what they have received.

□ This exercise may be used in combination with Peace–dove–crow–black (7.6) and Keywords II (8.11).

8.11 Keywords II

WHAT TO DO

1 As in Keywords I, choose a short prose passage with a relatively rich vocabulary load. Here is an example:

> The house endures.
>   Under the palm-fronds, under the wind, signed by rain with marks of a daily kind, like time. It has stained the timber walls with trails of black and slimegreen. The stilts on which the house stands drop pale gobbets of themselves on the chicken-raked mud. In the high wooden steps to the veranda the termites feed.
>   The palms above the house submerge the rooms in their surf of sound. Creakings and susurrations drop from the air. The palms wander in the bare wooden passages, in the gaunt living

room wide open to the sea. Sudden gusts send them streaming, grey-green plumes against a grey-blue sky.

Time has not smoothed or mellowed the fabric of the house. Grey splinters fur the walls of the central room, where maps and ships' pennants fade to a neutral dun. A smell of mildew circulates, from chests and cupboards where clothes, bedding, papers moulder in the hot damp.

The grass mats shine a little in the greenish light from the shutters. They show the path of someone who walks day after day between the windows, who leans day after day on the splintery sills to watch the sea.

A house is a castle; it defends. A house is a conch.

Under the palms, the house lies turbulent and still.

(Randolph Stow, from *The Visitants*)

2 Students again work individually, listing all the words which strike them as especially evocative or important to the overall sense of the passage.

3 This time the task is to *reconstruct* the passage as a poem. This does not mean copying it out word for word with breaks between lines. Instead words and phrases from the passage should be used to make a creative reconstruction of the passage. This will often involve omission of detail or re-arrangement. Here is an example:

The house endures,
Like time.
It stands, stained by rain,
Stained by black and slime.
Its stilts disintegrate
And termites eat its feet.
The palms above
Submerge the rooms
In a surf of sound.
The smell of mildew
Wanders in bare wooden passages,
And papers moulder and rot
In the greenish damp.
Under the palms,
The house lies
Turbulent –
And still.

4 Students exchange their poems with a partner and try to improve on what they are given. Then they discuss their proposed improvements in pairs.

COMMENTS

1 Although all students will be working on identical material initially, what they eventually produce will vary significantly from person to person. This provides rich opportunities for explanation and justification in the discussion stage.

☐ This exercise may be used in combination with Prose into poem (7.12) or Keywords I (8.10).

Some further ideas

So far in this chapter we have set out detailed instructions for a largish number of creative writing activities. Clearly there are very many more ideas which could be explored. Here are ten of them in outline form only:

1. Poems based on objects.
   Any of the following can lead into a poem:
   - How does it feel when you touch it? What does it smell like?
   - What sound does it make, if any? Does it have a taste?
   - What does it look like when seen from different angles?
   - What uses can it be put to? (Both usual and unusual.)
   - What relationships does it have with other objects?
   - Think of something as opposite to it as possible (e.g. a stone/water).
   - Get inside it. Try to feel as it might feel (e.g. a leaf, a stone, a piece of paper). What thoughts might it have?
   - What memories does it set off in your mind?
   - Make a proverb of it.
   - Use it to advertise something or write an advertisement for it.
   - Make a gift of it.

2. Poems based on special occasions (e.g. *the opening of a new swimming pool, the retirement of a colleague* etc.).

3. Poems based on people's professions. That is, projecting oneself into another person's work experience – its advantages and disadvantages, its pleasures and pains (e.g. *an interpreter, a bus conductor, an air hostess, a bank clerk* etc.).

4. Poems based on chance observations or experiences (e.g. *an incident glimpsed through a train window, a chance remark overheard in a bus, a sudden feeling of well-being or depression for no special reason* etc.).

5. A poetic will. What and to whom you would bequeath your possessions. This can be extended imaginatively by including characteristics, experiences and natural phenomena (e.g. *To my son I leave*

the smell of autumn apples – see Robert Lowell's translation of Villon).

6   Poems on the death of a close friend, a family member or a public figure. ('In Memoriam' poems are a recognised poetic subject.)

7   Poems based on old photographs, and the thoughts they provoke (e.g. Ted Hughes' *Six Young Men*).

8   Poems about a scar you have on your body – the memories and associations it sets off.

9   Poems on other people's irritating characteristics (e.g. D. H. Lawrence's *The Oxford Voice*).

10   Poems on hands and what they have held. (The *lightest, heaviest, oldest, newest, coldest, hottest* etc. things.)

An hour's work

Below are two examples of how activities could be combined for a session lasting about an hour. A brief explanation is given of the purpose of each exercise, with an indication of how long it might last. The first is for less advanced, the second for more advanced students.

Pre-intermediate–intermediate level

1 Missing words (2.2) or Missing lines (2.4).

   This is a useful 'starter', particularly with large classes and groups not used to working with poetry. The task of filling in a few missing words in a poem is easy enough for most students to cope with, yet hard enough to demand concentration.
   Time: 10–15 minutes.

2 Tangles (2.12)

   This requires more active participation from students. They are given the words of a short poem, but not the text. Before seeing the text, they try out various combinations of their own. This is a useful confidence-builder for weaker students: finding combinations is not difficult, and most will 'work'. The students are also gradually getting used to the idea of 'breaking into' a poem.
   Time: 10–15 minutes.

3 Word webs (6.1)

   The students are now ready for a more demanding exercise. In Word webs they gradually build up from memory – individually, then in groups – a list of words they have heard. These are then grouped according to association, and finally worked into a short poem. Here the students progress step by step from closely controlled towards freer expression. This gradual approach ensures that no-one gets lost on the way or left behind. In this exercise, the skills are well balanced between *receptive* (listening and speaking) and *productive* (speaking and writing).
   Time: 20–25 minutes.
   Note: The thinginess of things (6.8) could be used equally well here, and would take about the same time.

An hour's work

4 Expression (4.7) or Taking turns (4.11)

One or two short exercises which do not require too much thinking are needed to round off the hour. The reading aloud of a poem such as *Mornings* (see p. 102) or *The Pessimist* (see p. 106) would suit this purpose well. If time permits, a longer poem such as *The Prince* (see p. 98) could be used instead.
Time: 10–15 minutes.

Intermediate–advanced level

1 Using pictures (1.1)

Select one of the several ideas given in Using Pictures (1.1) or in *The Mind's Eye*, Maley, Duff and Grellet. The picture(s) chosen should have some bearing on the theme of loneliness or isolation. An exercise using pictures is chosen because later, in the role-play exercise (3.8) the students will need to visualize the poem.
Time: 10–15 minutes.

2 Immediate reactions (1.2)

The students are given a stimulus word or phrase, e.g. *loneliness, good neighbours*. They note their associations, compare notes in groups, then in the round-up session discuss any unusual items and any further ideas.

The purpose of this exercise is to set the students thinking around the theme, uninfluenced as yet by the poem. Many of the ideas which come up now will be of use later in the role-play.
Time: 10–15 minutes. (The first two stages should last together about 25 minutes.)

3 Dramatisation/role play (3.8).

The activity is based on the poem *A Sad Song About Greenwich Village*. The students first read the poem, then, in groups of four, prepare the roles of *old woman, neighbour, two journalists*.

Students are often asked to comment on poems about which they have little to say. Here, the traditional approach is reversed. The students begin with their own thoughts, move on to the poem, and from there to new ideas. The poem is not neglected, but it is also not made the *sole* point of discussion.
Time: 30 minutes.

Bibliography

Standard anthologies

Allott, K. (ed.) (1950) *The Penguin Book of Contemporary Verse*, Penguin Books.

Cecil, D. and A. Tate (eds.) (1958) *Modern Verse in English 1900–50*, Eyre and Spottiswoode.

Gardner, H. (ed.) (1972) *The New Oxford Book of English Verse*, Oxford University Press.

Harrison, M. and C. Stuart-Clark (eds.) (1978) *The New Dragon Book of Verse*, Oxford University Press.

Hayward, J. (ed.) (1956) *The Penguin Book of English Verse*, Penguin Books.

Heaney, S. and T. Hughes (eds.) (1982) *The Rattle Bag*, Faber and Faber.

Larkin, P. (ed.) (1973) *The Oxford Book of Twentieth Century English Verse*, Oxford University Press.

Lucie-Smith, E. (ed.) (1985) *British Poetry Since 1945* (revised edition), Penguin Books.

Morpurgo, M. and C. Simmons (eds.) (1974) *Living Poets*, John Murray.

Morrison, B. and A. Motion (eds.) (1982) *The Penguin Book of Contemporary British Poetry*, Penguin Books.

Stallworthy, J. (ed.) (1977) *The Penguin Book of Love Poetry*, Penguin Books.

Summerfield, G. (ed.) (1970) *Junior Voices 1–3*, Penguin Books.

Summerfield, G. (ed.) (1970) *Voices 1–3*, Penguin Books.

Thorpe, M. (ed.) (1963) *Modern Poems*, Oxford University Press.

Webb, K. (ed.) (1979) *I Like This Poem*, Puffin Books.

Anthologies of selected poets

Abse, D. and J. Robson (eds.) (1973) *Modern Poems in Focus 1–4*, Corgi Books.

Alvarez, A. (ed.) (0000) *The New Poetry*, Penguin Books.

Henri, A., R. McGough and B. Patten (1967) *Penguin Modern Poets 10*, Penguin Books.

Henri, A., R. McGough and B. Patten (1983) *The Mersey Sound*, Penguin Books.

Summerfield, G. (ed.) (1974) *Worlds: Seven Modern Poets*, Penguin Books.

Bibliography

Surveys

Press, J. (1969) *A Map of English Verse*, Oxford University Press.
Thwaite, A. (1985) *A Critical Guide to British Poetry 1960–84*, Longman Group.

Special collections

Abse, D. and J. (eds.) (1986) *Voices in the Gallery*, Tate Gallery.
Bolt, A. F. (ed.) (1976) *Double Take*, Harrap.
Fowler, R. S. (1967) *Themes in Life and Literature*, Oxford University Press.
Opie, I. and P. (eds.) (1987) *The Lore and Language of Schoolchildren*, Oxford University Press.

Books about teaching poetry

Hayhoe, M. and S. Parker (1988) *Words Large as Apples*, Cambridge University Press.
Leach, G. N. (1973) *A Linguistic Guide to English Poetry*, Longman Group.
Roberts, P. D. (1986) *How Poetry Works*, Penguin Books.
Tunnicliffe, S. (1984) *Poetry Experience*, Methuen.
Widdowson, H. G. (1975) *Stylistics and the Teaching of Literature*, Longman Group.

Teaching materials

Carter, R. and M. N. Long (1987) *The Web of Words*, Cambridge University press.
Gower, R. and M. Pearson (1986) *Reading Literature*, Longman Group.
Lach-Newinsky, P. and M. Seletzky (1972) *Encounters – Working With Poetry*, Kamp-Bochum.
Maley, A., A. Duff, and F. Grellet (1988) *The Mind's Eye*, Cambridge University Press.
Maley, A. and A. Duff (forthcoming) *Mirror Images*, Edward Arnold.
Maley, A. and S. Moulding (1985) *Poem Into Poem*, Cambridge University Press.

Materials for speaking/acting out poems

Graham, C. (1983) *Jazz Chants*, Oxford University Press.
Malkoc, A. M. (1984) *On Wings of Verse*, USIA Washington
Stibbs, A. and A. Newbold (1983) *Exploring Texts Through Reading Aloud and Dramatisation*, Ward Lock Educational.

Woodland, E. J. M. (ed.) (1966) *Poems for Movement*, Evans. Reprinted 1984, Bell and Hyman.

General reference

Cohen (ed.) (1960) *Penguin Dictionary of Quotations*, Penguin Books.
Drabble, M. (ed.) (1985) *The Oxford Companion to English Literature*, Oxford University Press.
Espy, W. R. (ed.) (1986) *Words To Rhyme With Rhyming Dictionary*, Macmillan.
Fergusson (ed.) (1983) *Penguin Dictionary of Proverbs*, Penguin Books.
Kirkpatrick, E. M. (ed.) (1987) *Roget's Thesaurus*, Longman Group.
Stillman, F. (1972) *The Poets' Manual and Rhyming Dictionary*, Thames and Hudson.
Tripp (ed.) (1976) *The International Thesaurus of Quotations*, Penguin Books.
Wilson, F. P. (1970) *The Oxford Dictionary of English Proverbs*, Oxford University Press.

Acknowledgements

The authors and publishers are grateful to the authors, publishers and others who have given permission for the use of copyright material identified in the text. It has not been possible to identify the sources of all the material used and in such cases the publishers would welcome information from copyright owners.

Orient Longman Ltd and Veena Seshadri for the poem on p. 14 from *I'm Not Like That and Other Stories*; A. D. Peters and Co. Ltd for 'Vinegar' by Roger McGough on p. 15 from *Modern Poets 10* published by Penguin Books Ltd; Deborah Rogers Ltd for 'Poem for Roger McGough' on p. 15 and 'Without You' on p. 118 by Adrian Henri; ADAGP Paris/DACS London for the Giacometti sculpture on p. 18; Robert Wallace for 'Giacometti's Dog' on p. 18 © 1968 by Robert Wallace; Geers Cross Advertising Ltd for the illustration on p. 21; Century Hutchinson Publishing Group Ltd for 'Childhood' by Frances Cornford on p. 24; John Foster for 'There are four chairs round the table' on p. 28, first published in *A Fifth Poetry Book* by Oxford University Press; Faber and Faber Ltd for the extract from *The Bog People* by P. V. Glob on p. 31; Faber and Faber Ltd and Farrar, Strauss & Giroux for the extract from 'The Grauballe Man' by Seamus Heaney on p. 31 from *North*; Carcanet Press Ltd for 'Spacepoem 3: Off Course' on p. 34, 'One Cigarette' on p. 64 and 'A View of Things' on p. 118 from *Poems of Thirty Years* by Edwin Morgan; Carcanet Press Ltd and New Directions Publishing Corporation for 'The Artist' on p. 36 and 'Landscape with the Fall of Icarus' by William Carlos Williams on p. 60. from *Pictures from Brueghel* © 1961 by William Carlos Williams; Routledge, Chapman and Hall for the extract from *Brideshead Revisited* by Evelyn Waugh on p. 37; Macmillan Publishing Company for 'Breaking Windows' by Vachel Lindsay on p. 38 © 1914 by Macmillan Publishing Company, renewed 1942 by Elizabeth C. Lindsay; Alan Brownjohn for 'In This City' on p. 40 © Alan Brownjohn; Random House Inc. and Harold Ober Associates for 'Dream Deferred' by Langston Hughes on p. 41 from *The Panther and the Lash: Poems of Our Times*; Harper & Row Publishers Inc. for 'At the Bomb Testing Site' on p. 42 from *Stories That Could Be True: New and Collected Poems* by William Stafford © 1960 by William Stafford; Patricia Pogson for 'Snowdrops' on p. 43 from *New Angles* Book 2 compiled by John Foster, published by Oxford University Press; John Murray for the extracts from 'The Highwayman' by Alfred Noyes on pp. 46 and 91–2 from *Collected Poems*; Tavistock Publications Ltd and Pantheon Books for the extract from *Knots* by R. D. Laing on p. 50; Faber and Faber Ltd for the extract from *The Conference of the Birds* by John Heilpern on p. 51; A. P. Watt Ltd and Macmillan Publishing Company, New York for 'When you are old' by W. B. Yeats on p. 54 on behalf of Michael B. Yeats and Macmillan London Ltd; Michael Swan for the translation of 'The Panther' on p. 57, and for 'Pity' on p. 62 and 'News Item' on p. 75; Faber and Faber Ltd and Random House Inc. for 'Musée des Beaux Arts' on p. 60 from *Collected Poems* by W. H. Auden; Faber and Faber Ltd and Doubleday for the extract from *Seneca's Oedipus* translated by Ted Hughes on p. 61; Routledge and Kegan Paul Ltd for 'The Coming of Winter' on p. 68 from *A Celtic Miscellany*, translated by K. H. Jackson; Martin Secker & Warburg Ltd for 'Coat' by Vicki Feaver on p. 72; Ian Serraillier for 'Prisoner and Judge' on p. 73 © 1973, 1976 Ian Serraillier, Longman and Puffin Books; Carcanet Press Ltd and New Directions Publishing Corporation for 'This is just to say' by William Carlos Williams on p. 74 from *Collected Poems, Volume I: 1909–1939* © 1938 by New Directions Publishing Corporation; Mori Cameron for 'The Atomic Tests at Bikini' from *Point of Departure* by James Cameron on p. 82; *The New Yorker* for 'A Sad Song About Greenwich Village' by Frances Park on p. 85 and the extract from it on p. 70 © 1927, 1955 The New Yorker Magazine Inc.; Artemis Cooper for the article on pp. 87–90; Oxford University Press and The British Council for the illustration on p. 92 from *The Highwayman* by Alfred Noyes and Charles Keeping, published by Oxford University Press 1981 and 1983 © Charles Keeping; Vasantha Surya for 'Advice to the Heart' on p. 100; Catherine Woods for 'Widowhood' on p. 102, first published in *Weyfarers*; McClelland and Stewart Ltd, Toronto for 'All there is to know about Adolph Eichmann' by Leonard Cohen on p. 104; Gerald England for 'To M.M.' on p. 108, first published in *Orbis*; Tim Dowley for 'Island' on p. 109; Martin Secker & Warburg Ltd and Viking Penguin Inc. for 'Reflections at Dawn' by Phyllis McGinley on p. 116, © 1957 by Phyllis McGinley, renewed 1985 by Phyllis Hayden Blake, first published in *The New Yorker*; W. H. Allen & Co. for 'I like that stuff' by Adrian Mitchell on p. 120; James McGibbon and New Directions Publishing Corporation for the extract from 'Faces' by Stevie Smith on p. 121 from *The Collected Poems of Stevie Smith* (Penguin Modern Classics); Bernard Young for 'Lionel' on p. 138, first published in *Orbis*; Donald Stubbs for the illustration on p. 168; Museo del Prado for the illustration on p. 170; Buckau Wolf India Ltd for the advertisement on p. 172; Somersham County Primary School for the photograph on p. 173; Jonathan Cape Ltd and Viking Press Inc.

Acknowledgements

for the extract from *Voss* by Patrick White on p. 174; Martin Secker &
Warburg Ltd and Richard Scott Simon for the extract from *The Visitants*
by Randolph Stow on p. 175.
  Artwork by David Stubbs.